Lady
in the HOOD

Dorothy Moore is a dramatic extension of what happens when a person with a good heart, sharp mind, and track record of achievement yields to an even greater Heart! Her passion and unflagging zeal in pursuing the well-being of the broken, needy, hungry, and hurting has borne the fruit of lives turned around, souls transformed, and precious human beings recovered unto wholeness, giving them a future and a hope. Her story speaks of the possibilities and potential in any environment when the "well-heeled" give themselves to see others well healed.

—Jack W. Hayford
President, the Foursquare Church

Here she comes: meet the Lady in the Hood—Dorothy Moore. I met Dorothy in a friendly, unassuming gathering in Dallas. She was most gracious and very humble, welcoming everyone. When she heard that I, along with my late husband Gordon Lindsay, were cofounders of Christ For The Nations, working with thousands of young people from around the world, we became steadfast friends as we visited back and forth. Dorothy's love for the down-and-outers of all ages and all races was apparent. She invited me to eat with her in downtown Dallas in rundown buildings she had acquired to house men, women, boys, and girls with needs and problems of every kind and even of a very serious nature. Whatever was needed, in whatever location, Dorothy made the move: food, clothing, housing, and teaching them of Jesus and their need to change their lives through His love for them. No finer example will any reader find than this account of Dorothy Moore's personal story. You will be recommending it to your family and friends.

—Freda Lindsay
Cofounder, Chairman of the Board Emeritus
Christ For The Nations, Inc., Dallas, Texas

I had the honor of nominating Dorothy Moore of Dallas as an Unsung Heroine. Dorothy founded Reconciliation Outreach Ministries in 1987 to help inner-city street kids with the East Dallas Crusaders program. Her shelter serves as a safe haven for teens, as well as for women, men, and children of all ages. Dorothy began her shelter with very few resources and an abundance of hope and determination. Community organizations and local corporations opened their hearts to Dorothy. She brought together the many individuals and organizations who worked to make the dream of the shelter become a reality. Because of Dorothy, hundreds of homeless people in Dallas have a roof over their heads, a meal on the table, and the love of a caring neighbor in their hearts. She has mastered the skill of nourishing both body and soul with her understanding and dedication.

—Texas Senator Kay Bailey Hutchison,
from presentation at U.S. Senate
"Unsung Heroines Award Recipients,"
February 16, 1999

Lady in the HOOD

Dorothy Moore
with David Yeazell

CREATION HOUSE
HOUSE
A STRANG COMPANY

LADY IN THE HOOD
by Dorothy Moore with David Yeazell
Published by Creation House
A Strang Company
600 Rinehart Road
Lake Mary, Florida 32746
www.creationhouse.com

Unless otherwise noted Scripture quotations are from the New King James Version of the Bible. Copyright © 1979, 1980, 1982 by Thomas Nelson, Inc., publishers. Used by permission.

Scripture quotations marked kjv are from the King James Version of the Bible.

Design Director: Bill Johnson
Cover designer: Marvin Eans

Library of Congress Control Number: 2008923862
International Standard Book Number:
978-1-59979-365-8

08 09 10 11 12 — 987654321
Printed in the United States of America

DEFINITIONS

Lady \lā-dē\ n: A woman of superior social position;
a woman of refinement and gentle manners
—Merriam-Webster Online Dictionary[1]

The hood \hůd\ n: shortened form of
"neighborhood;"
often implies a ghetto or urban community
—The Online Slang Dictionary[2]

ACKNOWLEDGMENTS

To the Lord, who gets all the credit for the changes in my life and the work of the ministry, I give my grateful praise! Without You none of this would have been possible.

To my wonderful family, who has loved me through all the years of this story. You continue to be the most important part of my life. To all the Reconciliation Outreach staff, volunteers, board members, and supporters, and the foundations and community organizations that have supported the mission's work over the years. Thank you for sharing your time, talents, and finances.

To all those who helped me write: David Yeazell, who assisted me in bringing together and focusing the years of information and history into this final manuscript; Susan Heard and Glenda Brannon for input on content; Shawn Sturm for graphic design and formatting; and Giles Hudson for input on promotion. The story would not have been written without your assistance.

CONTENTS

one

THE EARLY YEARS

The fourth child of Harold and Helen Engh, I was born on July 25, 1935, in Sycamore, Illinois. They called me Dot. The nickname came from my birth name, Dorothy Anne. I was a complete and unexpected afterthought to a family that already had two teenage daughters and one twelve-year-old son.

Little Dot

Although I wasn't planned for, I never doubted my special place in the family. From the start, my position was secure. As the baby of the family, I was loved and doted on, like a little princess, by both parents and siblings. My father, Harold Viking Engh, was a fiery Norwegian whose nickname at work was "HV" or "High Voltage." Born in 1893 in Chicago, the son of poor immigrants, he moved to Sycamore, Illinois, my mom's home city, in 1915 to work as a maintenance man for the Insulated Wire Company.

My dad, the aviator

Dad's was the classic Horatio Alger story. After a tour of duty as a World War I aviator flying biplanes over France he returned to Sycamore, and through hard work, aggressiveness, and ambition eventually rose from sweeping the factory floors to become company president. My mother, Helen Wittimore, born three years after my dad, was a woman with a great deal of personality, full of fun, joy, and just plain lovely to look upon. Her father was a banker from an old, moneyed family who traced their lineage back to one of the first families in the original thirteen U.S. colonies. The honor of such pedigree, for generations of female Wittimore descendents, has been membership in the elite Daughters of the American Revolution.

Against the wishes of his future in-laws, dad convinced my mother to marry him. Granddad and Gomma (grandmother) Wittimore were not happy with the immigrant boy—an unacceptable son-in-law, a newcomer to a land they had called home for centuries, a factory worker marrying a banker's daughter. Despite my grandparents' initial displeasure, they eventually agreed to the wedding.

A vindication of my dad's worth as a son-in-law came after the great stock market crash of 1929. When my grandfather Wittimore lost a fortune in the market, it was my father who came to the rescue and bailed Granddad, becoming forevermore a favored son-in-law!

My father was a very strong leader and a dedicated family man. Despite his leadership abilities, he wasn't very good at teaching me the value of money. As a girl, I remember him telling us that we needed to be careful with our spending; his idea of saving money was to use his paper napkin twice.

During the early years of their married life, Dad worked hard at the factory, while Mom birthed and cared for my three older siblings: Jean, who was sixteen years older than me, and Barbara, a year behind Jean, and Harold Jr.

Following a merger of Dad's company with the much larger, New York-based Anaconda Wire and

Cable Company, my father took a new position as Executive Vice President. Our family packed up and moved from the cornfields of Sycamore to the East Coast. We found the perfect home in Irvington, a thirty-minute train ride north of New York City.

SLEEPY HOLLOW

Irvington, New York, was a wonderful, almost magical, place to grow up. My family lived just up the road from Washington Irving's home, Sunnyside, a quaint, renovated seventeenth-century Dutch farmhouse, complete with a gabled roof and located on the Hudson River. The house had not yet been turned into a museum and was deserted during my childhood. I spent many afternoons exploring the grounds and peeping in the windows looking for the Headless Horseman and Rip Van Winkle.

Since I was a great deal younger than my siblings, I grew up like an only child, and I enjoyed the rare privilege of being alone much of the time. Everything was an adventure for me. In my fearless independence, I explored the worlds of books and nature. The brook that ran from the hills above our home to the Hudson was one of my favorite places—the long branches of a partially fallen willow tree providing Tarzan vines to swing across to the other side.

Dot crossing the brook

My nanny, Annabelle, suspected the worst when two friends and I disappeared one afternoon while playing down at the brook. We floated pencils downstream and got them stuck in a small culvert while trying to reach the Hudson. Hours later we met up with a frantic search party that, unbeknownst to us, had been sent after us. Annabelle and the other adults were exasperated, but I was undaunted. That brook never lost its charm for me.

Washington Irving's tales followed me to the Sleepy Hollow Country Club. The Headless Horseman rode there, and so did I, on a highly intelligent horse that followed my every command.

In the indoor ring I spent seemingly endless time doing practice in dressage, a form of equine competition. Outside, I was free to fly down the trails on the old Rockefeller estate. It was there that I discovered the wonder of effortless motion, mounted on that huge animal. The horse and I became as one cantering along the miles of beautiful bridal paths. I never quite belonged to the town of Irvington since I did not attend the public school. My grade school years were spent at the Hudson River Children's Country Day School in Dobbs Ferry, where my favorite person was the cook, Tillie, who always "took up" for me in my frequent bouts of discipline handed down by the firm hand of the headmistress, Miss Darling—her real name, by the way.

My worst punishment was the loss of the solo in our Christmas program. I had escaped study hall by climbing out the window of the old school house onto the roof. All was well, until a parent drove up and reported seeing my feet dangling over the gutter.

I also managed to get myself in real trouble when I accidentally dropped an open bottle of glue in the toilet. It overflowed and we watched in amazement as the water poured down all three flights of the school's carpeted stairs.

During those early years, I did have a couple special friends. One of them was a red-headed boy, the son of the local fire chief. We were the perfect pair, I, with my sense of adventure, and he with his street wisdom, gained by following his father around the community.

He and his father's fire truck had to rescue us one winter when I forgot to turn off the phonograph; it shorted out and started an electrical fire in the basement. Instead of evacuating the house with the rest of the family, I followed the fireman and my friend Buddy back into the basement to watch the stream of water that put out the flames.

LIFE ON BROADWAY

One end of our property, 41 North Broadway, was bordered by a tall stone wall that separated us from Broadway—the same street with all the theaters in New York City. The early suburbanites came in their carriages from New York on Broadway as it wound its way north following the Hudson River. Later, the commuter trains followed the same path to Westchester County and beyond.

Our house on Broadway

My closest friend, Nina Puckett, lived across Broadway, high above me near a castle. Our favorite method of communication was a high-pitched, shrill yodel, probably similar to the one used by my grandfather's Viking ancestors. Another friend, Lucy McGregor "Greg" Williams, lived just down the road from us. She and I hung out together from childhood, going ice-skating in New York City with my nanny in the winter and, in the summer, visiting my home in Illinois. We were the best of pals. Greg and Nina were always close by my side when I got into mischievous behavior.

One of our favorite activities was to explore the two castles just up the hill from us. One was deserted and never seemed to mind our visits— our entering and leaving via a huge round pipe that may have been a sort of fire escape for the second floor. For some reason, I was always the princess in the tower, with Nina stuck in the role of the hero who rescued me from endless perils.

The other "castle" was a very odd, large estate with lots of sheep and cattle and no electric lights. Two unmarried elderly sisters lived there— descendants of a Dutch sea captain named Rutter. They always seemed to enjoy our visits, as we were ceremoniously led into a dark hall lit by kerosene lamps that created huge shadows on the dark paneled walls. We would then climb three flights of stairs to stand on the widow's walk on the roof, with its perfect view of the Hudson River. The top floor of the house was my favorite, a complete aviary with over one hundred varieties of stuffed bird life. Before we left, the sisters usually offered us tea and cookies. The older of the two then went to a cabinet and opened the bottom drawer to display, before our wondering eyes, a lock of Abraham Lincoln's hair!

THE CREATIVE ENTREPRENEUR

As a girl I had an active imagination. The large attic of our house was my special world where I, with the help of my friends, pursued my juvenile professional and business interests. At one point the attic housed my hairdresser's shop. I took a lamp and hung cords from it, placing clips at each end to look like what I had seen in the beauty shops of the day. I then put the contraption on my friend's head, turned the light bulb on, and fried her hair.

It was in the attic where Greg and I established a floral shop. We went around and picked our neighbor's flowers; brought them up to my "shop;" cleaned, arranged, and wrapped the flowers in silk; and went door-to-door, reselling corsages to the same neighbors we had stolen the flowers from earlier in the day.

I also had a doctor's lab in that attic, collecting specimens for my lab work and hiding them in the attic eaves. Years later as an adult I revisited my family home. In our discussion of my childhood, the family who then owned the house complained of a strange smell in the attic whose source they were unable to locate. With a smirk on my face, I took them to the attic and introduced them to the Dorothy Engh Research Lab and the secret stash of amazingly preserved specimens.

MERRY OAKS

Mother and Dad never lost their love of Sycamore, so every summer when all our friends left New York City for exotic places like Fire Island and Cape Cod, off we went to the cornfields of Illinois. The property was entered by driving down a long lane lined with trees. Merry Oaks, our summerhouse, was outside town in the woods—and merry it was with four hundred acres of woods, cleared land for the big brown house, and later, our own swimming pool, tennis court, two-hole golf course, and skeet range.

The Engh Family at Merry Oaks

The house was spacious and felt like a rustic hunting lodge with its two-story living room and upstairs balcony connected to our bedrooms. A huge stone fireplace ran from the first floor upstairs and all the way down into the basement. The upstairs had a sleeping porch with screened windows that stretched all across the south side of the house. Many nights we all slept on that porch, enjoying the cool of the night air. Once again, similar to my experience in Irvington, I did not quite fit in with the Sycamore kids—although I enjoyed lots of company as I invited anyone I met in the grocery store to come home for a swim. Mother never knew who I might bring home next, but it was a wonderful way for me to meet all types and colors of people, and I took advantage of the situation.

In 1947, during my seventh-grade year, my father was asked to be president of the Pyle-National Company in Chicago, and we permanently moved back to Illinois. Due to the move, I skipped the seventh grade and began the eighth grade in Sycamore.

My favorite part about the move was learning about rural life: the Future Farmer's of America and the Grange, with its square dances and potluck suppers. We also owned the farm across the highway, and I had the fun of collecting the freshly laid eggs from the henhouse and riding on the tractor with the farmer.

A favorite memory of my mother was during my teenage years on one of our frequent trips to downtown Chicago. I had begun to play the role of a rather sophisticated young lady, and Mother, in her inimitable way, burst my bubble as we were walking down Wabash Avenue. Looking up to the sky and tall buildings, she said in a loud voice, "Would you look at those tall buildings, Dot? Wow, isn't this something!" I was so embarrassed my face turned bright red. It was only later that I understood her sense of humor and her great understanding of me.

After one year in Illinois, my parents sent me back to prep school. It was at The Masters School in Dobbs Ferry, New York.

EARLY SOCIAL CONSCIOUSNESS

As a wealthy, white family in the 1930s and 1940s, our household ran smoothly because of the hard work of our black servants: Jonas and Cora Brown. Living in the servant's quarters of our house, Cora was the cook and Jonas the chauffeur and gardener.

Dad and Mother with Jonas and Cora Brown

My mother hired staff who had worked for other prominent families so she could learn how to buy the socially appropriate silver and china to fit in with the well-heeled crowd. Due to my parents' extensive international business travels, Cora, Jonas, and my nanny, Annabelle—who raised me starting at age two—became my family. The family ties carried on over the years. When Annabelle eventually married, she asked my father to give her away and me to be the flower girl. The wedding, a time of special bonding between all of us, was my first experience in an all-black church. The family ties continued when, following sixteen years of faithful service, my parents bought Cora and Jonas a retirement home. The influence of Jonas, Cora, and Annabelle on my life went way beyond their service of cooking and cleaning. It planted in me a foundational questioning of issues of racial and economic justice that later influenced me as an adult in ministry. As a child, they shared the pain of their segregation and poverty with me, telling stories of rejection at the hands of the broader society because of the color of their skin. Cora, who was a lighter-skinned mulatto, shared with me about not fully fitting in to either black or white society. As a young girl, I was affected deeply by my experiences with them, developing within me my first feelings of compassion for people who experienced pain or lack.

Annabelle and Dorothy at family picnic, 1942

During the one year that I attended public high school, I sang with a music group. One boy in the group, Joe, was black. When we traveled out of town for concerts, I again became aware of the depth of discrimination when our black team member

15

was barred from certain hotels and restaurants because of the color of his skin. It made my team members and me very angry, and we decided to boycott any place that wouldn't accept all of us. As a young girl, I often rode the train from my private school into New York City, passing through Harlem on the way. Several times I got off the train in Harlem and walked up and down the streets trying to understand a place and people that were foreign to me.

On one of my Harlem visits, I forgot to take money with me. I had to borrow a dime from a man on the street to use the public phone to call my parents to ask them to wire funds to the Western Union office so I could get home.

Even as a high school freshman, I tried to grasp the difference between my privileged life and the lives of those living in what is now considered the inner city.

REBELLIOUS YEARS

Like many youth, I went through a rebellious stage. In the relatively tame 1950s, I partied, not by doing drugs, but by bending the rules. I constantly pushed against the constraints that were present in my life in order to have the freedom to do what I wanted. I was attempting to find my identity, make sense out of life, and find an outlet for my high level of creative energy.

In high school I returned to The Masters School in Dobbs Ferry, a strict boarding school just north of New York City. I was regularly in trouble, but never enough to be thrown out of school. During my senior year at Dobbs, I participated in the Westchester County Debutante ball at Sleepy Hollow Country Club. My date, Dudley Lucas, was an old friend and heir to the International Paper Company. After the initial ceremonies and shaking of hands, Duncan and I decided it would be more fun to go to the attic and empty a trash barrel full of beer cans onto the asbestos below while the formal party continued. We did so until my father noticed my absence and sent people throughout the building to find where his daughter had disappeared. Duncan and I came sheepishly back to the ball and behaved ourselves the rest of the night.

I also remember a date with a boy from Dartmouth. He was a rather proper young man, and I decided to burst his bubble. I arrived on the date wearing a three-quarter length fur coat and bermuda shorts. He was aghast. Instead of taking me out to a nice restaurant, he ended up taking me to the local diner to buy breakfast.

In the course of the evening, I convinced him that I came from a poor farm family from Illinois. Six months later I was an attendant in a coming of age party in Chicago for a friend of mine from Northwestern University. At the reception, this same young man saw me, pulled me out of the reception line in a fit of rage, and wanted to know what I was doing there and why I had played him as a fool. I am not sure what my motives were, except to poke fun at the social mores of the day. At Dobbs, I led a raid on the kitchen, where we found a large vat filled with peanut butter. A couple of my friends held me by my feet as I dangled precariously over the vat, scooping out cupfuls of peanut butter and handing it back to the other girls. Unexpectedly, the lights went on in the kitchen and my friends dropped me headfirst into the vat and ran. Of course, I ended up being the one in trouble, and it took days to wash the peanut butter out of my hair.

During a school break my friend Sally and I went to Montreal to board a ship for a two-month trip to Europe. On the spur of the moment to avoid sitting around waiting for my ship, I decided to take a cruise of the shoreline. It wasn't until after it launched that I found out I was on a two-day cruise. The only problem was that my ship for Europe was leaving in the morning. They had to take a lifeboat and catch up with the cruise ship in the bay to get me back to the Europe-bound ship.

London was the first stop on our grand European summer tour. Sally and I stayed in the Brown Palace Hotel on Bond Street in the financial district. After we unpacked, we did some laundry, hanging our clean undies on a clothesline stretched between the bathroom door and the knob on our window.

I quickly finished dressing, and, forgetting about the clothesline, slammed the bathroom door. The elastic on the doorknob snapped and the whole line acted like a slingshot. Aghast, we watched our underwear fly through the open window and float down twenty floors to the sidewalk below. At just the right moment, a very dignified British gentleman looked skyward and spotted the unusual items. Without so much as a change of expression, he stuck his umbrella up and impaled the bras and underwear.

"Sally," I said, "let's get out of here before he gives the underwear to the desk clerk. I don't want to be in the room when they find our names neatly sewn in each item" (like all good prep school girls do). She agreed and we quickly left the room.

As we got off the elevator, there was our British gentleman telling his story to the bellhops. We quickly became the brunt of a great deal of British humor. One of the clerks asked if this was the American way for girls to get attention.

COLLEGE

My first two years of college were at Sweetbriar in Virginia. I believe that my parents sent me there in an attempt to make a lady out of me. My roommate, Bobbie Sue, who I totally ignored, came from Odessa, Texas, a state that I would later call home.

At the time, I believed I had nothing in common with her because I was the product of Ivy League,

East Coast snobbishness and all she talked about was the university. We eventually became good friends. In fact, her brother, Jack, was our neighbor in Highland Park, Texas, years later. I finished my two final years of college close to home at Northwestern University in Evanston, Illinois. The first year at Northwestern, I lived with my sister and her husband since there was no dorm space available. Bobbie became like a second mother to me, and her family and I have continued a close relationship to this day.

When I entered Northwestern, I had never been in a co-ed school, except during my eighth grade year in Sycamore. I signed up for an Ancient Greek history class and was amused on the first day of class to see a room full of huge, muscular boys. What were they doing in a Greek history class? I soon discovered that the whole football team was in that class because they knew the professor would give them all passing grades so they could maintain their place on the football team.

At Northwestern, I started to major in music but eventually switched to English. I'm not sure what I expected to do with an English major, as I didn't want to teach or be a secretary. My father once told me that the only thing a woman could be was a teacher, a nurse, or a secretary. My attitude was that I would die before doing any of those things. In school, I never even took a typing course just to be sure that I would never be qualified as a secretary. And, although I genuinely liked kids, I didn't want to teach them. During spring break of my junior year, my friends and I decided to drive to Ft. Lauderdale, Florida, for the week. On our return trip north, we ran into severe winter storms and didn't arrive back in Illinois until the wee hours of the morning. The dorms were not open, so we decided to go to my sister's house. Because my sister and her husband were on vacation, we parked the car in the driveway of her home and went to sleep. The next thing I remember was the glare of police searchlights shining through the car windows. Explaining to the police that I was the sister of the homeowner was to no avail; my sister and husband had left the children with a baby-sitter who didn't know me and thought we were thieves. Finally my nephew Doug roused from sleep, leaned out the window to check out the commotion, and yelled, "Aunt Dot, what are you doing?"

WESTWARD-BOUND

When I finished my senior year at Northwestern, California sounded like a glamorous place to live. My roommate Gail from Northwestern was already there with her family, so off I went across country, alone, in my orange convertible.

21

Dorothy in California, 1959

I decided the safest way for me to drive was to follow the big truckers. I stayed behind large trucks the whole way to California. For a break, I pulled into a truck stop, where a trucker teased me for following him. I told him I was safe behind his big truck. I landed my first job in San Diego as a receptionist with KGB Radio. I was in the right place at the right time. Because of my music background, the station manager allowed me to program the music and help establish their new FM station.

During my time at the station, I even got an opportunity to host my own show and help with local news. One time I heard about a police raid on the police band and followed the raid out to the docks. At the site, the police had the murder suspect cornered, and I, with microphone in hand, got a firsthand interview on the raid. Back at the station, they gave me a commendation for not getting shot.

Soon after my arrival in San Diego, a handsome naval officer moved into our apartment complex. He was a typical Texan, complete with bowlegs and a Texas accent.

Bob Moore in dress whites

At the time, I thought that all Texans had horses, lived on a ranch, and played the ukulele. When Bob courted me with his ukulele, I decided he was the right one for me, a true Texan and a strong man that I could respect and depend on. Following six months of dating, our two cultures joined—West Texas with the East Coast—when we were married on October 3, 1959, in Sycamore, Illinois. Bob told me he would bring me back to Texas, tame me, and keep me barefoot and pregnant. He managed to do the pregnant part. I believe that I was looking for someone like my father, a man who worked hard for what he had, a definite strength of character that I found in Bob's life. Prior to meeting Bob, most of the guys I dated had been given everything on a silver platter. I was a self-willed and rebellious young woman and knew that I could control a weak man.

Bob was everything my Ivy League boyfriends had not been—hard working, dependable, and intelligent; but our cultural differences and temperaments were worlds apart. He was a tough-minded, West Texas boy who never really had a childhood, while I was a poor little rich girl who did not want to grow up.

Our wedding, 1959

My parents gave us an engagement party in Chicago. After the party, Bob and I went to an outdoor concert at Ravinia. In preparation for the celebration, I accidentally packed one white shoe each from two different pairs, one a spiked heel and one a mid-height heel. I had to spend the entire evening with a limp.

We spent the first night of our married life at the Edgewater Beach Hotel in Chicago. Because Bob forgot to register me in at the hotel as his wife, when we arrived at the room the desk clerk turned to me and smiled at me with a knowing look. Beginning with that first night, as a couple we were probably as ill-prepared as any two people could have been to understand each other and to bridge the gap between us. Bob really knew nothing of my childhood or lifestyle, and I nothing of his.

Much of my personal identity and significance came from my family. My father was an imposing and important man, and I was used to a very privileged lifestyle. On trips overseas we were waived through customs and never had to wait in the lines. In restaurants, the maitre d' always found us the best table. As a result of being accustomed to a lot of special attention and deference from others I had a shallow attitude about what was important in life. During times when I acted like an undisciplined, spoiled wife, Bob held his ground.

Married Life

For our first year of married life, Bob and I returned to San Diego. I continued to work at the radio station and maintained the social expectations of a Navy Lieutenant's wife. The following year we moved to Austin, Texas, where Bob entered law school at the University of Texas. My first experience in Austin was at a restaurant where the waitress said, "Honey, you're not from Texas, are you?" My clipped accent and bermuda shorts must have given away the fact that I was a little Yankee who had just arrived in the world of southern women—and a culture that was completely different from the East.

In time we made many new friends in Texas, including George and Gayla Chapman and Curtis and Patricia Meadows, and I began to enjoy being a Texan. Amazingly, our friends loved my outspokenness, and in time we rubbed off on each other and grew in our friendships. By the time law school was over, I was becoming gentrified, had joined the Lawyer's Wives' Club, and later became president of the Junior Bar Wives.

While Bob was studying, I worked as a social worker at St. David's Hospital in Austin. It was my first experience working with people in need, and I enjoyed the opportunity and the challenge.

As a young, industrious social worker, I remember interviewing a large lady who was holding her sides. She said she was in labor and I panicked. I had never had children, but knew she was about to have a baby on the hospital floor. I grabbed an attendant who put her in a wheelchair and rushed her up to emergency to deliver the baby.

During my break, I went upstairs to check on the woman. The OBGYN came out of the hospital room laughing; the woman I was convinced was having a baby in reality had a benign tumor, on, of all days, April Fool's Day.

THE FAMILY BEGINS

I worked at the hospital until our first child was born. Our son, Robert Clay Moore Jr., arrived at 27 weeks after a terrifying two months of nearly losing the baby. We were visiting Bob's family in West Texas when my water broke. The doctor put me in a local hospital, where I stayed for a week. Bob had to fly back to Austin for his law exams, and I lay in the bed watching my first dust storm. The sky turned dull gray and the dust was everywhere, even coming under the windowsills.

Mother flew from Chicago to help me get back to Austin. It took a wheelchair and a hoist to lift me up into the plane, but we made it home. Once in Austin, I was confined to complete bed rest, unable to tend to our first new home, while my husband sat in exams.

When I finally did go into labor, Robert, or as we

called him, Clay, was born with pneumocystis and was unable to breathe on his own. At the time, I wasn't a believer and it never occurred to me to pray for him. Fortunately, our pediatrician was a Christian and came to the hospital, baptized Clay, and prayed for his healing. Later, the same doctor drove me from Austin to Texas Children's Hospital in Houston in his own car.

For three months my husband and I lived in Houston to be close to the baby, who was still hospitalized in a research situation where people came in all day to observe his recovery. Those months in Houston while Clay was fighting for his life put a great strain on both Bob and myself emotionally and financially, but by some miracle Clay lived. He was so tiny that we took him home and dressed him with doll clothes from the toy store. In spite of his premature birth and illness, Clay is a strong, healthy adult today.

Holly, our Christmas gift, arrived the next year on December 15 during Bob's final law school exams. We had no money, and Bob was trying to be a father, husband, and aspiring lawyer.

Dorothy with Clay and Holly, 1962

After law school graduation, Bob took a position with the Atomic Energy Commission at the Argonne National Laboratory in Naperville, Illinois, where we lived for two years. We spent a great deal of time in Sycamore with my family, because Merry Oaks was like a childhood fairyland for all of us. My parents were able to play with Clay and Holly when they were small. When the kids first got up in the morning, my father would get them up and march them in their pajamas out to the pool, where Dad made them "walk the plank," jump in the pool, and swim to the other end.

During our years in Naperville, our family bonded closely to my sister Bobbie and her family, who lived in the area, and to my brother, Bud, who also moved back in the area to help my father out with a company that he had purchased in Sycamore. A special early memory was our first Christmas as a married couple with young children at Merry Oaks. The ground was covered with freshly fallen snow. We recruited a family friend to play Santa Claus, dressing him up in a red suit and providing a horse and sleigh from the farm. The horse and sleigh arrived in a snowstorm, and Santa, with bag of gifts over his shoulder, gave us all an unforgettable Christmas.

After only two years in Illinois, my husband convinced me to go with him back to his Texas roots, and we moved to Houston, where he was employed by Humble Oil, now Exxon. The kids were still very little and adjusted quickly to our new home.

In those early years I enjoyed the role of stay-at-home mom in our cute little house with a backyard covered with wisteria. Little did I know that God was getting ready to impact my life in a way that would forever change my world!

two

SPIRITUAL JOURNEY

After several years in Houston, Bob was contacted for an interview with Texas Industries in Dallas. Surprisingly, the assistant treasurer of the company was the husband of my best friend at Dobbs. Another friend from Irvington was married to the chief counsel of the company. Bob put the two wives on the phone, and then told me he had accepted the position.

We packed and moved to Dallas that fall, finding a home in University Park on San Gabriel Street. The children enrolled in Bradfield School, and I became involved with the Dallas Junior Bar Wives. We became good friends with several of our neighbors who were new attorneys with young children. We played tennis together as couples and had many happy times with picnics and family events in our backyards.

Dorothy, George Bush Sr., and Patricia Meadows

My back-door neighbor—now a lifelong friend—was my first experience with a Southern grande dame. Corinne Calder was originally from Shreveport, Louisiana, and entertained us regularly with some of the best cooking I have ever experienced. My first memory of Corinne happened the day we took possession of our house. I looked out the back window to see a strange woman pulling weeds in my yard. When I went out and introduced myself, she informed me that she expected me to keep my yard weed-free or she would be back!

During those years in Dallas I became immersed in the socially elite Highland Park crowd and deeply involved in the children's school activities and neighborhood events. At the time, I was so busy trying to fit in with the group that I had little opportunity to think about my own need to grow up or to deal with some of the problems that were developing in our home.

You see, my independent spirit stayed with me all through my youth. I had never bowed my knee to anyone, not my parents or school authorities, and after my marriage, certainly not my husband. I was a liberated woman long before the woman's liberation movement had a name. Only after twelve difficult, turbulent years of marriage did I begin to look outside myself for an answer. I had deliberately chosen a very strong-willed self-made man for a husband, and our clashes were frequent and loud. Our backgrounds were very different, and although we loved each other, we had to struggle through almost every decision to find any common ground to build a future together.

Bob was a west Texas pioneer who had worked his way through college on the oil rigs in the four corners area of New Mexico and in west

Texas, far from the comforts of home. The rough ways of the West were new to me, and it took many years for me to understand and respect the toughness and strength of character he represented.

I wanted to become a stronger woman and had tried to be a better person on my own, but it would take a real crisis to bring me to my knees.

I DIDN'T NEED A SAVIOR

Like so many other children, I went to church and Sunday school through my teen years and enjoyed the youth group and the singing. One of my close friends, Jinny Mellon, was the pastor's daughter. Church was a part of my social life, but had very little spiritual influence on me.

My family attended the Federated Church, a denomination similar to the Disciples of Christ. My parents never talked about their personal faith, but both of them lived their faith and set good examples for us. Dad gave generously to help others and Mother took me with her on many missions of mercy to help elderly relatives. She was always kind to our extended family and set a good example for us all.

As the baby of the family, I was too spoiled and mischievous to imitate my wonderful mother. My rebellious streak began to show, and I became somewhat of a free spirit. My father became my role model. I loved his booming voice and strong personality. He loved to sing, and by the time I was five he made me stand on our balcony and sing his favorite songs whenever they entertained guests. As a result, I developed confidence in front of a crowd at a young age. My confidence in myself grew as I experienced success, first as a singer and then as a championship diver. I loved the water, having learned how to swim after Dad pushed me into our pool at the age of three. Those small successes kept me busy. Though I began to discover myself, I still felt no need for God.

Like so many others who grew up in our Christian culture, I did pray, although I had no real relationship with the One with whom I was talking. The Bible was like a history book to me, and seeing only "nice" people in the church, I never experienced anything that challenged me to understand who God was or recognize my personal need for a Savior. When it came to college and the early years of married life, church was attended merely during the main religious holidays or when it was socially expedient. Church had no impact on my life until my family relocated to Dallas.

THE GREAT SURRENDER

After twelve years of marriage and four children, I was headed for the divorce courts when a friend of mine dragged me, against my will, to a Bill Gothard Basic Youth Conflicts Seminar. God spoke to my heart in the seminar through the scripture that was shared. The Bible's picture of marriage didn't look a bit like mine. As I listened to the Word, it came alive for me, and I was deeply moved. It was as if God Himself were speaking to me, and all I could do was listen as His voice brought a wave of love over me. I saw how hopeless my efforts at being a wife and mother had been and how much I needed God's help. I surrendered my life to the Lord and asked for His grace and strength. That day, I heard the Word of God preached with greater clarity than at any time in my life. The Word broke me, convicted me, and made me hungry to experience the reality and presence of God. It was after that pivotal experience that I began to seek after and learn about the things of God. I had experienced a drink of truth. I was thirsty and I wanted more!

When I surrendered my life to the Lord, the Spirit fell heavily on me, like a heavy blanket that pinned me to the floor of the bedroom. After the children left for school I spent hours on my face crying, but for the first time in my life I felt completely free.

That night, when I arrived home, I yanked Clay, Molly, Helen, and Kelsey out of bed, got them all on their knees and said, "You will all pray and ask Jesus to be the Savior of your soul." In obedience, they all jumped out of bed, got on their knees and prayed. Following that experience,

I fell so in love with Jesus that Bob actually was jealous. The Lord's presence in my life was all consuming, taking priority over everything else.

From the beginning, the children and I grew together in the things of God. Bob was gone overseas for weeks at a time on business, and the kids and I spent hours together in prayer and Bible study. The children knew from the beginning that a dramatic miracle happened in their mom. I remember our son Clay telling me that I was so different he knew I hadn't changed by myself, so it had to be God!

Even my conversion experience wasn't very traditional. Initially I didn't really understand that Jesus was the Son of God, nor did I know about the necessity of coming to Jesus to confess sins. In the beginning, all I knew was to surrender my life to God and ask Him to change me.

So, I committed all my life to Him and asked Him to teach me. Like Paul falling off his horse after meeting the risen Christ, I met God through the Word and with very limited understanding chose to follow Him.

In my initial experience of the Lord, I understood that I needed to be broken, not in terms of sin, but that my self-life had to break.

Over time, the Word of God convicted me. As I saw the standard of God and how far I was from that, it helped me to understand my own sin nature.

Through years of Bible study I began to understand that the Word became flesh and dwelt among us. (See

John 1:14.) The Word was telling me about a person, Jesus, who stood in my place and took my load of sin, guilt, and shame, sacrificing His life for mine so that I could be changed. His promise became real to me.

THE MEEKING PROCESS

I have always loved horses, and as a girl I spent hours with an old cowboy named Ruben during our vacations at Desert Willow Ranch in Tucson. Ruben would rope the mustangs that roamed the wild areas near the ranch and would bring them into the rodeo ring to meek them—breaking their will to the will of the rider so they could be useful.

Dorothy (center) barrel racing at Desert Willow Ranch

The memory of that helped me understand that the Lord was doing the same thing in my own life. For the first time, I understood that the God who had created me could also use my life for His purposes if I let Him. Surrender was hard for me. Obedience was not even a word in my vocabulary, so this meeking process was pretty rough at times.

The first Bible verse I memorized was Proverbs 14:1: "Every wise woman buildeth her house: but the foolish plucketh it down with her hands" (KJV). The next one was Proverbs 15:1: "A soft answer turns away wrath." The Bible promises if you continue in His Word, then you are His disciple; you'll know the truth and the truth will make you free. (See John 8:31–32.) I was amazed that truth could be so simple when I had spent my first thirty years fighting against it! From the day of my salvation experience, my life was totally transformed. One minute I was willfully going a direction of my own choosing; the next moment I only wanted to do what God wanted in my life. God had gotten a hold of me. I knew from the moment He touched my life that total brokenness was the only answer, and I began to grow spiritually. I remember the battle inside, as if it were yesterday. The old me still wanted things my way. Many a night I lay, face down on the carpet, fighting with my desire to run.

It was God's way, not mine, one day at a time. I had a seven-year honeymoon with the Lord, a relationship that so completely transformed my life that all I wanted was more of Him. I didn't work outside the home, so I had plenty of time for Bible study and prayer, and a wonderful mentor,

Ann Lawson from Highland Park Presbyterian Church, gave me a crash course in Christianity. All the stuff I had done in my life suddenly seemed silly and frivolous. Most of my life had been totally focused on having a good time. I expected others to take care of me and never wanted any responsibility. Once God got my attention, I began to recognize the selfishness of my lifestyle. It was a great shock! It has taken me years to undo all the old mind-sets, snobberies, judgmental attitudes, and harshness.

After my encounter with Christ, I began to attend Highland Park Presbyterian Church, and, for the first time, the good news of the gospel had a meaning of its own for me and my children. I met many wonderful people during my early years in Highland Park. I am always thankful for the Bible studies with Navigators, a ministry with a focus on discipleship, who taught me the Word and how to apply it to my daily life.

BAPTISM IN THE HOLY SPIRIT

In 1974, a headhunter approached Bob to become vice president and general counsel of a new geophysical corporation formed in Houston. Our family was uprooted and we moved south, far from the security of my Christian friends. I felt as though I had lost everything. I was taken away from the cocoon of love and training that I received through the Navigators to a whole new situation.

Moore family, early 1970s

Bob was gone almost constantly, negotiating contracts overseas. I was trying to find myself and my place as a Christian.

At that point in our married life, my husband was able to earn enough money to provide a comfortable life for us. Money had always been very important to me. The irony was that when Bob became successful, I wasn't interested; I was newly saved and all I wanted was to be a missionary and lay down all those worldly things.

I remember flying one year with Bob on a corporate jet to Paris and the Bordeaux country. I deliberately chose to wear a frumpy cotton dress on the plane, because I was attempting to come to grips with my own snobberies and struggles with money. It seems silly to me now, and perhaps I was full of self-righteousness at the time, but, in reality, I knew I needed to change.

In Houston, we attended St. Andrews Presbyterian Church, where Bob and I began to grow under the teaching ministry of Dr. Harper, the pastor at St. Andrews. The church was open to the gifts of the Holy Spirit, and approximately a year after we moved to Houston I experienced the baptism in the Holy Spirit.

Early on in my walk with the Lord, I began to read about Francis Hunter and others in the charismatic movement and even visited several charismatic churches. Even though my initial impression was that they were silly, I could clearly see the operation and power of the Spirit of God through these ministers. I knew that I didn't have, nor did I understand, what they had.

My attitude change began after I read Catherine Marshall's book called The Helper, which described her relationship with the Holy Spirit. I trusted Catherine and had read everything that she had written. If she believed in the baptism of the Holy Spirit, that was good enough for me. I went into my closet, closed the door and asked the Lord to baptize me with the Holy Spirit.

What I experienced was less than satisfactory to my mind. In answer to my prayer, I received what seemed to me a silly, unemotional prayer language that sounded like pig latin. It certainly wasn't dignified or beautiful. I decided that if this was all there was to this experience, I didn't need it, and that was that.

One day I was driving my car with all the windows closed and shouting at the Lord concerning a crisis I was facing. Suddenly, I began to speak words through my nose in a high-pitched, nasal language that sounded like an oriental tongue. God used that incident to break my resistance. I then heard an inner voice asking me, "Are you too proud to use what I gave you?"My instant response was, "No, Lord," and I began to use the "foolish" words in my prayer time. The Scriptures say that "God has chosen the foolish things of the world to confound the wise" (1 Cor. 1:27); looking back on this time in my life, I realize that God was using those experiences to help me deal with my pride.

In the beginning, I even recorded the language to try to understand it. Today, my prayer language is a very important part of my life and ministry, and I continue to pray with my understanding and with the Spirit.

BEGINNING MINISTRY

My earliest sense of God's call to ministry took place as others began to ask me to pray for them and as I was asked to teach Bible classes in people's homes and churches.

The very first time I taught was at a women's seminar called Eve Reborn. The event ended up being my first encounter with spiritual opposition, making me realize how important those seven years of preparation had been. Thankfully, I had the confidence to handle the situations I faced.

During the first class I taught, a lady stood up in back of the church and verbally attacked me on the topic I was teaching. She was very angry and began to argue with me concerning a statement I made about submission. I answered her questions as quietly as I could, but she would not back down. She later called me on the telephone, screaming at me, using dirty words that I didn't even know she knew how to pronounce. She manifested an ugly side that I had never seen before. The situation brought me to my knees. It was a difficult challenge for a young minister, but God used that experience to teach me a foundational truth that helped me keep focused during years of ministry.

The truth I learned was that not everyone was going to love me just because I had a good heart. That there would always be opposition, and that opposition may come from places we don't expect—the body of Christ.

An early incident in Houston foreshadowed later ministry: I walked into the middle of a gang fight on the way to a store. A group of boys were repeatedly beating a boy as he lay in the street bleeding from several deep cuts on his face and arms. I walked up to the leader, got right in his face, and said, "In the name of Jesus, stop! You were not raised this way. Your mother taught you better than this." The boy looked at me in total shock, let go of the other boy and sauntered off.

As the gang dispersed, I followed the boys into the pool hall nearby. I talked to each boy individually, handed each a gospel tract, and told them that Jesus loved them and they needed to pray and ask forgiveness for what they had done. One of the leaders of the gang broke down and asked me to pray for him to get right with God. That experience showed me that God could give me the boldness to do things that were completely out of character for me.

Aglow

I received the majority of my early ministry training from Women's Aglow, where I learned about the work of the Holy Spirit, spiritual warfare, and how to use the gifts of the Spirit. The training was timely, necessary, and useful, since my whole life felt like it was under a tremendous spiritual and emotional siege. The battle was multifaceted— in my children, marriage, and in my ministry.

During my years with Women's Aglow, I traveled as a speaker, teaching primarily in the area of deliverance. That was not a subject I chose to teach, but it became the primary topic as I gained experience in ministering freedom to individuals that were bound by the enemy.

At a retreat in south Texas, somebody called me to a cabin where seven women were sitting on a woman who was out of control. Her body was thrashing about with unusual force and power. I walked in the cabin and commanded the spirit to loose her. It was like watching a balloon deflate, as she immediately quieted down and the ladies were able to get off of her. I stood there, amazed at the power of God and the way He used me to help the woman. I was so new to the ministry of deliverance that I had no idea what to do next. I asked the Lord, "You have delivered her, now what do I do?" Through that circumstance I began to understand how to take a person through deliverance and help them recognize the issues that allowed the demon's initial entrance into their lives. I learned to ask the Lord to fill the empty place with the Holy Spirit and to begin the process of what is called inner healing.

At the time, I became involved in the inner healing ministry, training under a Baptist couple, Earl and Betty Sue. They became mentors to me and began to allow me to pray with them in their services.

Ministering with them, I saw for the first time the manifestations of the Holy Spirit, including people healed of depression and more serious demonic problems that were often generational and behavioral. Through these experiences I began to discover my own gifting in this area and began to operate in a level of discernment and knowledge that I had never before experienced.

I had many fruitful years of ministry with Aglow. Lives were touched through teaching and personal ministry, and I grew in my understanding of ministry to the oppressed. On an Aglow ministry trip to Corpus Christi, Texas, the Lord spoke that the cloud had moved and that He wanted me to move with it. The Lord showed me that the anointing was moving, and that He wanted me somewhere else. He had to shake my teeth out to separate me from that ministry. God used some significant upheaval and personality conflicts within our Aglow chapter to move me into my next season of ministry and to further refine my character.

HOME MINISTRY

For the next few years, our home became a ministry center. In the evenings, people came in and out of our living room for prayer, ministry, and Bible study. We primarily worked with young adults between the ages of seventeen and twenty-five who were considered outcasts and rebels in society and were leading self-destructive lives. My own kids helped me at this time. Clay played the guitar while Holly and Helen helped with teaching. They each brought many of their friends home with them and a real fellowship began to develop.

It was during these informal times of ministry that God again taught me much about deliverance, spiritual warfare, and discerning of spirits, as I often didn't know how to deal with the spiritual bondages and problems in people's lives. During one evening of home ministry I prayed for a lady with serious mental problems. She was so overcome by God's presence that she fell into a chair in Bob's office and remained in that chair for over two and a half hours. When Bob came home, he walked in his office, saw the apparently passed out woman in his chair, and asked, "What on earth is going on?" When we finally got her up, her whole countenance had changed. She continued to attend the Bible study and was eventually reconciled to her family.

St. Andrews

The pastor of our Presbyterian church and his wife became our good friends. Dr. Hooper was perfectly suited to disciple and teach Bob and me.

Momma Bo was a large Catholic lady who floated into St. Andrews during our prayer meeting one morning. She pulled out her guitar and began to teach us worship choruses. For the first time I experienced the joy of worshiping God with my eyes closed. I began to attend her prayer group on a regular basis.

When the group began to sing in the Spirit, it was as if heaven came down and God began to dwell with us. Many of the women in the group had personal problems, as I did. But Nehemiah 8:10 came to life before me as we discovered that the joy of the Lord really was our strength as we celebrated and found joy in the presence of the Lord despite our struggles. I learned to enjoy Him even in the midst of problems. I began to teach an eighth grade Sunday school class in the recreation hall of our church. The first time I walked into the hall for class, they were sitting on the pool table playing craps. As usual, I was completely in over my head and began to pray for a breakthrough. As the new teacher, I wrote down each child's name, prayed for each one, and found that God began to move in the class. I raised the children's vision by telling them stories of what God had done around the world in missions. We ended up with a class of kids that were hungry for the things of God. Even the most rebellious child softened. I began to see that God had some plans for me working with children.

My pastor eventually started a ministry to the homosexual community and their families, and he began to refer people who asked for help to me.

My hairdresser was one that I ministered to in the homosexual community. Through our relationship and conversations in his beauty shop, he told me he had walked out of his marriage, leaving his family in New Orleans, and wanted help to restore his life. Finally, one afternoon he called and asked me to come pray with him. He was ready to leave his alcoholic lifestyle and male partner. I was caught off guard by the phone call, but hearing the urgency in his voice I rushed over to his house on my own. I knew better than to go alone into a ministry situation, however, in my excitement, I forgot. As I prayed for him, he was completely set free. In time, he left Dallas and returned to his estranged wife and family. After the deliverance session, I went to the neighborhood grocery and was walking back to the house. Crossing the street, I felt a sensation like a physical hand on my back that forced me facedown in the middle of the street. As I got up from the street, my mind was filled with dirty pictures, like watching an X-rated movie. I was really frightened, so as soon as I got home I went upstairs to my bedroom and locked the door. When the children arrived home, I told them I was sick and wanted to be left alone. I didn't know what to do or what I was dealing with, but knew I was being attacked spiritually and needed God's help.

I stayed in my room all night, speaking the name of Jesus and reading the Word. By the morning the confusion had lifted. I was back to normal but was very aware of the lack of wisdom in what I had done.

THE MINISTRY OF HEALING

My introduction to and training in the ministry of healing began under the guidance of a woman named Delores Winder. Delores was healed under Katherine Kuhlman's ministry and had a ministry of her own in Shreveport.

Prior to her healing, Delores was dying. Her nerve endings had atrophied, and she had been locked in a back brace for fifteen years, bedridden after the birth of her last son. Her husband drove her to a Kuhlman meeting in Fort Worth. During the service, she suddenly began to experience a burning sensation all over her body.

As Katherine Kuhlman called out the name of her disease and pronounced her healing, she began to walk, sliding her feet on the floor. A doctor came over to her and asked what happened. She told him that her legs were burning and wondered how she could feel in her legs when the nerve endings had been burned out. When Delores left the stadium, she went into the ladies' room, took her brace off, and instantly every vertebrae in her spine snapped into place.

Because of her dynamic testimony, Delores and her husband began to share her story and pray for the sick within the Presbyterian charismatic groups of the day. I met her when she came to speak at St. Andrew's Presbyterian Church. After the church service that night, Delores and I talked the entire night and she laid her hands on me to receive the anointing for healing. I was way too practical and logical to receive what she was trying to impart to me. I kept trying to figure it out. I finally experienced a breakthrough at 3 o'clock in the morning! I had been praying for a child who had epilepsy, and I got a vision of an old fashioned typewriter with the keys locked.

Through that vision, I saw the that the child's nerve endings were unable to release from a frozen position, just like those locked keys. From then on I began to see through new eyes. It was as if my eyes had been opened to see things and know things beyond my natural understanding. I traveled with Delores to many Presbyterian churches where Delores prayed for people to be healed, and many received. Delores insisted that I stay with her and continue to grow in my spiritual and ministry understanding. Delores believed that the Lord would help me to overcome the natural mental blocks in my mind.

The first healing I was allowed to experience took place in my kitchen. A friend, Isabelle, a Jewish Christian with tremendous back pain, was over for a visit. I laid my hands on her for healing. She slid down on the kitchen floor, then, leaning on the stove, got up and had no more pain. That was the breakthrough that encouraged me to continue ministering to others and to leave the results to God.

Many wonderful manifestations of God's healing grace have happened over the years. Perhaps the most unusual was a lady from the mission who had been diagnosed with uterine cancer. I prayed for her in her hospital room just before surgery, and when they brought her back to the room the doctor said there was no evidence of cancer. We all celebrated God's goodness right there in the hospital.

THE WORD OF KNOWLEDGE

The first time the Lord spoke a word of knowledge to me for another person happened during an Aglow prayer meeting. I was serving as the president of Aglow at the time and the Lord spoke in my spirit concerning Isabelle (the lady whose back had been healed at my house),"Because she now believes me, she will receive what she had asked." I thought that because I knew Isabelle so well that this was a natural thought on my part and I didn't need to tell her.

The next day in another prayer meeting, Helga, the guest speaker from Dallas, came to Isabelle, laid hands on her and said word for word, "Because you now believe me, you will receive what you have asked." From there on I learned to let go of my own understanding and trust the Lord to teach me things.

At another Aglow meeting, a lady came to me for prayer for the healing of arthritis, and the Lord said she had bitterness toward her mother. I asked her how her family relations were and if there were any problems. The lady replied that there were no problems. I then said, "How about your mother?" The lady then confessed, "I haven't talked to her in fifteen years."

As I have learned to trust the Lord to speak through me, the word of knowledge has flowed. Often, when ministering, I walk to the platform and receive insight and discernment concerning the people in the room. Over the years, a growing spiritual discernment has helped me in the selection of our staff and leadership. The Lord has protected me from all sorts of things by showing me people who can be trusted.

OBEY WITHOUT QUESTIONING

During my years in Houston, I learned to follow the Lord without questioning Him. One year, I flew to Los Angeles for a Women's Aglow conference where David Wilkerson was the main speaker. On the second day of the conference, I heard the Lord say, "Pack your bags, change your ticket, and go home!"

The request seemed odd, as I hadn't received a phone call from anyone back home. I argued with the Lord, reasoning that David Wilkerson was speaking that night and I had come all this way and spent money to hear him speak. The response from the Lord was total silence.

I obediently packed my bags, headed out to the airport, got on the next available flight, and took my seat next to a man working on his computer. Almost as soon as I sat in my seat, putting my Bible down, the man turned to me and said, "You have something you need to tell me, and I'm going to put my computer away and listen."

For two hours we talked. I shared the Lord, led him to Christ, and watched him as he wept for joy right in his seat. I arrived home and found that everything was all right. The experience was simply a divine encounter that reinforced my need to obey Him when He speaks.

PASSING OF THE BATON

From 1983 to 1985, I attended Bible college. I completed my first year at Southern Bible College. The following year, the school moved to Oklahoma City, so I transferred to Gulf Coast Bible College, where I graduated with a bachelor's degree in Christian counseling and a deep love for the Word of God.

In the faculty, I saw a commitment to pass on a heritage to the students. I primarily learned from Dr. Elizabeth Williams, Academic Dean at Southern Bible College, who became my personal mentor. Elizabeth singled me out my first year of Bible College. We spent a great deal of time together, and she spoke an unusual destiny into my life. She told me that she knew that I had a calling, not to be a teacher but a pioneer. A woman of God with great intellect, Elizabeth spoke and lived a life of godliness with authority and dignity. She was a pioneer as a woman in ministry. She was both a missionary and a college professor who embodied the presence of Christ in her life and provided me with an inspiration and example that I wanted to follow in my own experience.

During a church service at Evangel Temple in Houston, the minister came out of the pulpit to me and said there was an older woman, Elizabeth, who was handing me her baton—an anointing from God—and that I was to run the race in my generation.

Little did I know that the baton would soon take me even further outside my comfort zone, calling me to minister across cultural, racial, gender, and economic lines in a dangerous, drug and gang-infested neighborhood of east Dallas.

three

THE CITY CALLS

In 1982, Bob once again received a call from Bob Rogers, now president of Texas Industries, who asked him to return to the company as vice president and general counsel. Bob accepted the position and we packed up and returned to Dallas for the second time. Both Bob and I were excited at the opportunity to return to what we considered home. This time we found a house in far north

Dallas close to some friends from Texas Industries. The neighborhood was very different from our former Dallas neighborhood of Highland Park.

Moore Family, 1980s

My time was completely committed to the things of the Lord during the ten years of my time in the Houston area. In looking back on my move from Dallas to Houston the second time, I realize that the Lord had to remove me from all the things I had become attached to in Highland Park in order to do the things He did in my life during those years away. Our stay in Houston was a time of preparation for me socially, emotionally, and spiritually. I was in a completely different environment and could not depend on old friendships or social relationships.

By the time we moved back to Dallas the second time, I knew that I needed to separate myself from many of the old ways of life that I had become attached to during the first time I lived in Dallas. My identity had been derived from the social relationships that I had there. The Lord now wanted me to grow on my own into a woman who had the freedom to cross the cultural boundaries that separated the inner city from my old way of life.

When we came back to Dallas, I was afraid that I would be caught up in the social whirl again, but instead I found that most of my old friends had gone on with their lives. This left me the freedom to establish a new identity on my own.

We began to attend the newly formed Hillcrest Church, a nondenominational congregation under the leadership of Morris Sheets. My call to the inner city came shortly thereafter as I joined a group of Hillcrest members who were actively praying about reaching out to the inner city of east Dallas.

A couple from Hillcrest Church, Mark and Cara, and their sixteen-year-old daughter, Ginny, had moved into an east Dallas neighborhood with a burden to reach out to their neighbors. A team formed to support their outreach efforts by holding a crusade in their neighborhood. We began with three months of walking the streets in the area and praying, although the violence and ever-present drug dealers gave us a real challenge.

THE TENT CRUSADE

During the Texas state fair, we leased a vacant lot on Virginia Street, put up a tent for the adults and one for the teenagers, and began a two-week tent crusade. At the time, Virginia Street was a melting pot of cultures: blacks, Latinos, a few whites, and a wave of families from Cambodia and Vietnam.

The teen tent was the result of my special burden for the youth. They needed their own style of Christian music and a chance to relate to others their age in a Christian setting. Those who came to share with them were not all young, but they identified with the struggles of youth and could relate to their needs.

The neighborhood children came after school each day and the fun began with songs and Bible stories, followed by a food line. By 5:30, people began drifting over to the lot, drawn by a group of young people playing guitars and singing. Operation Blessing brought food to give away and others brought clothing. We went to the tents after the meal and began the service.

During the first week of the crusade, I noticed a man across the street from the tent who was sitting on the stoop of his house with a baby on his knee and a bottle of bourbon in his hand. He watched us during the entire crusade and was there again the second and third nights.

I finally got the courage to go across the street and try to talk to him. Although he was drunk at the time, he looked at me when I began to talk and said, "Thank God you're here. For the first time, my little girl is safe, and she is able to cross the street and join with your music without my worrying about her. I know I'm not living like I should; but I'm glad you're here, and I hope you'll stay."

The second week of the crusade, a man came rushing up to me in the tent, grabbed my arms, fell on his knees, and said, "I ain't gonna do it anymore." I looked down at him and said, "You ain't gonna do what anymore?" "I ain't gonna take the clothes and the bread that were on your flatbed truck and sell it in the next block. Will you please forgive me? I ain't gonna do it anymore," he replied. Only God could have convicted the man, as none of us had any idea of what he was doing. He later became one of our best helpers as we established a long-term neighborhood group that continued to fellowship together over the years.

In the first week of the meetings, most of the neighborhood kids stayed outside the tent listening from a safe distance, some lounging on cars parked nearby, the younger kids leaning on their bikes looking cool and street-hardened. We used huge amplifiers to carry the music to the streets. People literally hung out of their apartments to hear what was going on. A young woman fresh out of prison, Laurie, told her story of abuse and drugs, then told the kids how Jesus and His message of hope had helped her let go of years of bitterness and begin life again. The first person to come inside the tent was a hard-looking Hispanic girl about fourteen years old who responded to the love of Christ that night. The adult services were in English, but were interpreted into Spanish by Pastor Roberto and into the Cambodian language by Pastor Nopal. The ministry teams and the people who attended were a cross-section of cultures. A real spirit of fellowship developed, and those who came felt the special love that existed between all members of the ministry teams.

In one of the meetings, Connie Martinez, a graduate of Teen Challenge who had a local ministry to Hispanic gangs, was scheduled to share her testimony, but didn't make it to the meeting. I had no choice but to come to the front and lead the meeting. I turned it over to the Lord, prayed fervently, and began to preach. The best way I can describe it was that I slid into something that I didn't have control over—the words flew out of my mouth. There were three kids that came up to the altar that evening and asked us to pray for them.

One night when I was speaking, two Asian teens came forward to receive Christ. I motioned for help from the Cambodian translator, who quickly discovered that the youth were Vietnamese, not Cambodian. As I started to pray for them, this high-pitched, nasal language came out of my mouth, and I began to speak in an East Asian tongue. The boys began to cry; they understood what I was saying. With the help of the Cambodian pastor, we took them to a Vietnamese family who had a fellowship in their home.

One of the individuals I invited to the crusade was Nadine Gimball. Nadine lived in the Roseland Homes government housing project and worked at Win Lee, the beauty shop where I had my hair done. Nadine brought all of her kids to the crusade, and, in time, became a co-laborer in ministry. In the spring of 1988, Nadine and I organized an anti-drug March through Roseland Homes. One hundred persons carrying big placards walked the streets proclaiming the name of Jesus.

During the march, we noticed that the local police were following close behind the marchers. At the time, we did not know that there were death threats against me from the local drug dealers. The march went on without incident, and it ended in an outdoor crusade, where Nadine gave her testimony of salvation and deliverance from drugs.

March in Roseland Homes, 1988

AFTER THE TENTS CAME DOWN

By the time the crusade ended and the tents came down, several hundred church members from six churches and Christ For The Nations Institute had been involved in its ministry. Hundreds of pounds of food were shared every night with the hungry. Thirty different laypeople and pastors preached, and many more shared their own personal testimonies. Boxes of literature and Bibles were given away, along with loaves of bread and clothing. Music groups, drama teams, mimes, and dancers came to share their talents in the adult and teen tents each night.

Following the outreach, the ministry to the teens continued. We had a core of kids that continued to return. During the weekdays, Nancy Gibbons worked with the youngsters. Every Thursday, I worked with the teens in Connie and Mark Gibbons' house, where a church was being birthed. The Gibbons' home had been open almost continually since the crusade began, and they held a worship service on Sunday afternoons. My group consisted of a tiny core of black and Hispanic teens. We were an unlikely bunch—I, teaching; and a soft-spoken, gentle American Indian student from Christ For The Nations, the son of a Navajo medicine man, playing the guitar. The kids kept coming back week after week, and the group grew larger as new kids came with their friends.

Early in our interactions, the Lord showed me that the older kids needed a gang to offer them a sense of belonging and purpose, an alternative to the violence and drug-infested option on the streets. The newly formed "gang" adopted the name East Dallas Crusaders for Christ. Sensing a need for a permanent presence in the inner city, I incorporated Reconciliation Ministries in 1987.

Members of the crusade teams continued to work with the people in the neighborhood as the need arose. Several of the men found jobs with the help of team members. One team member, Jeff, did carpentry work for various church members, providing on-the-job training for several of his Spanish-speaking friends.

Many of the people in the neighborhood went with the Gibbonses on Monday evenings to help feed the street people. Those who had received help were learning to help others.

THE HOOD

Let me digress from the storyline for a moment to give you a clear picture of the geographic area the Lord had assigned us to. Based on our research before the crusade, the area we chose had the highest crime rate in the city. At the time, the neighborhood was the demographic drug-drop center for Dallas, complete with rampant violence and multiple murders. It was a neighborhood where police raids were common, ambulances rushed; sirens blaring to pick up those shot; and crime scene tape cordoned off crime scenes.

The majority of the housing in the area, except for some poor families, was the habitation of drug dealers. They were everywhere, including all the houses that the ministry eventually took over. Drugs, gang violence, and graffiti were everywhere you looked.

For those unfamiliar with urban slang, the term the hood is a shortened version of "the neighborhood." I actually ministered in the hood for a couple years before I understood the terminology. One night as I stood outside our rented building on Haskell I began to think about the meaning of "our" hood. It was a neighborhood filled with poverty that produced tough young people who learned how to take care of themselves in any way they could. As I began to pray for the area I looked up at the Beer-and-BBQ sign above my head, and in my mind the sign changed to a picture of Jesus with His hands outstretched. Under

His feet appeared the words "Jesus in the Hood."

Early on we had about half Hispanic and black teens with a small minority of Asian and Caucasian teens. However, beginning in the mid 1970s, the east Dallas neighborhood was a destination for many new immigrants from Asia. We had many Vietnamese, Cambodian, and Laotian families.

The Asian gangs and rivalries were strong. The Amer-Asian kids, many born from the union of American dads and Asian mothers, were the most angry and violent. From them, we regularly found graffiti over our office door and received actual death threats.

Our quieter Asian children were often over-whelmed by the verbal and demonstrative communication style of the American kids. To minister to this varied Asian community, I found a child in each culture group who could speak English. The translator helped me as I visited various apartments to gain permission to take a family's children to camp. I remember entering the dimly lit apartment of one Cambodian family and sitting down on their sofa—and right on a chicken!

I once taught a Vietnamese man to drive. I thought he had driven a truck in his home country, but he spoke very little English. I soon learned he knew nothing about trucks or cars. He was short in stature and had to sit on pillows to see over the steering wheel. We got in the car, and I told him to put his foot on the brake; instead he pushed both the brake and the gas pedal to the floor. I told him to take his foot off the gas and instead he released the brake. We flew through the parking lot, and just before we hit the pastor's car head-on, I managed to pull on the emergency brake. That was the end of my driver's training work. From then on I sent them to driver's education class.

The Asian culture I observed exhibited genuine community. Tightly knit and family-oriented, they did everything together. For those of us working with them, it was a real cultural education, and I learned to respect these hardworking, kind people.

LOST IN THE HOOD

The Crusaders lived all over the inner city, and we had to pick them up after school and take them home at the end of the night. In the beginning, we followed a route into south Dallas and the projects that took almost an hour. We used my large Suburban and two other cars. I would pull up in front of Nadine's apartment in Roseland Homes and the fun began as the kids piled in on top of each other, sitting on each other and on the floor. When we arrived at the ministry, the kids seemed to multiply when we opened the door.

I am not known for being good with directions. During the early days of the Crusaders, I took a wrong turn and got lost late one night in south Dallas when I was returning the kids home. I got stuck in a dark alley and couldn't find my way back to the interstate.

There was a group of men loitering in the alleyway, and I felt vulnerable, as if there were a spotlight stuck on me. Eventually I got my courage up, prayed, rolled down the window, and asked one of the men standing in the alley for directions. The man was nice, turned me around, and gave me directions to the freeway. Then he said, "Little lady, if I were you, I would lock my door and get out of here as fast as you can!"

DANGER IN THE HOOD

For all the years of ministry in the inner city, we were never touched by all the murder, rape, and kidnappings in the area we were called to serve, although we often found ourselves right in the middle of potential danger.

One day the Lord told me to walk up to a man standing at a pay phone. He was dressed in a white mink coat. I boldly approached him, told him my name, and said that I had come down there to do ministry. He said, "Honey, you are out of your territory and over your head." When I got back to my car, the rest of the team informed me that I was talking to one of the biggest drug dealers in the area.

Even so, I walked into several situations where drug battles were going on. One night as I got into my convertible, a drug dealer being chased by the police ran directly in front of my car. To avoid the bullets flying over my head, I slid down in the front seat of my car.

Several times, while taking the Crusader kids back to their homes in the projects, I walked into the middle of gang or drug activity. One night, Nadine and I were talking out by the clothesline in front of her apartment in the projects. Nadine had been taking clothes down while we were talking and praying for the children. As we were talking, a man came running by, stopped at the clothesline and dropped something into Nadine's clothespin bag. As the police chased the man, Nadine and I took the clothespin bag into the apartment and found a package of drugs. The following day we took the drugs to the police.

I also made numerous trips into crack houses to get permission from drug-addicted mothers to take their children to the doctors. In a very rough section of Roseland Homes there was an apartment set aside for the drug addicts. I entered into a very dark and smoky room. The oppression was so heavy that it made you want to stop breathing in the air of the room. There was an overwhelming sense of heaviness standing among so many people who had reached a place of no hope.

When I asked for a particular mother, the man who answered the door took me to the dining area in the back. Fortunately, the mother agreed to sign the papers so I could take her son to the doctor.

Several times we had parents sign over legal rights to medical care and school. Entering crack houses became less uncomfortable over time. I realized that if the Lord sent me there, He would go with me there, so I never felt afraid. I remember meeting one mother in south Dallas near a recreation center. There had been a season in her life when she attempted to change, but she had since relapsed into addiction and risked losing any rights over her children. When she arrived, I pleaded with her that there was still hope and a chance to turn her life around so she wouldn't lose her kids. At the time, her little boy, seven or eight-years-old, was regularly taking a glue-soaked rag up to his face and inhaling the fumes to get an instant high. The mother held onto me and wept, but she still made the choice to walk off into an empty field. I said good-bye and never saw her again.

YWCA

To keep our gang of Crusaders from heading back to the influence of the streets, we recognized that we needed to have multiple opportunities for activities, training, and exposure to the world outside the inner city. From 1987 to 1988, we found a home for the Crusaders at the YWCA, where we partnered on a feeding program and summer camp.

I was joined at the Y by two friends, Nancy Beth Roberts and Gina Harriston. Nancy Beth recalls those initial years together:

When I came on board it was just
Dorothy, with her white, blond hair and
blue eyes—a New York debutante; I,
who was just as unlikely as Dorothy,
driving into East Dallas in my white
Jaguar; and Gwen Harrison who,
disabled, walked with a cane and used
a breathing apparatus. Dorothy, in fact
all three of us, were an unlikely group
to begin a ministry that flourished. I
believe there were other people that
were His first choice, but because
we three were available and willing,
although unlikely, God used us.

While we were meeting in the YWCA, Tarus,
a boy with major family problems, came to
Crusaders from the projects. Tarus and his siblings
saw their mother shot in front of them. At the
time he started coming to Crusaders, around the
age of nine or ten, he lived with his grandmother,
who was running a prostitution ring. He also had
drug dealer uncles coming in and out of his life.

One morning he came early before the
others. He ran up to me, fell on his knees, and
wrapped his arms around my legs. He begged
me to help him learn to control his terrible anger.

Sure enough, an incident happened with Tarus
later that same year. One of the Hispanic boys

had insulted an African-American girl in front of Tarus. Tarus reacted immediately and pulled a shiv (knife) out of his sock and chased the boy around the Y, eventually backing him into a corner. A near riot broke out and someone called the police.

I was in the gym teaching a Bible study when the police came and got me. They had Tarus in a room separated from the other boy. I went to him and asked him to give me the knife. Big tears spilled down his cheeks as he handed me the knife and said he was sorry.

Tarus came back to me later and said that because of what he did, he knew he had ruined everything for me and that I could never go back to the Y. While we lost our house at the Y, the incident had a positive effect. I realized that we needed more time with the kids if we were to make any real difference with the deeply troubled ones.

From the Y, we temporarily moved to a recreation center close to Baylor Hospital. In a desire for a more permanent location, we then moved to a long, narrow office on Bryan Street. We paid a rent of four hundred dollars a month. Our very first building was a dark, windowless space between a bakery and the office of Save the Children. Since we met after school, the area was clear and the kids could make as much noise as they chose without bothering the neighbors.

I had no idea where the money would come from for the rent that first year, but somehow between a merciful landlord and a generous husband we made it. Nancy Beth says it best:

> Dorothy stepped out in faith and took the first lease—one little section of where they are now on Bryan. At the time we didn't have the funds or credibility. Dorothy did a lot of it out of her own pocket, as no foundation would pay attention to her.

Nancy Beth and I were given permission to have a noon counseling session for troubled kids at Spence Junior High in East Dallas. The only room available was the science lab, which became our center of operations.

The teachers who knew us would send their troublemakers to us during the lunch hour. The first group of Hispanic boys arrived in two gangs ready to kill each other. Things got off to a rough start when one of the boys, Antonio, found the gas jet used for science experiments and threatened to blow us up. I took him aside and demanded he sit down, and then I bowed my head and prayed out loud. Soon the room was quiet and all the boys bowed their heads and joined us.

Little by little they began to trust us, and many of the gang followed Antonio to the East Dallas Crusaders to learn more about God's love.

During those early years we took our kids to the first summer camp. We offered what we had, which wasn't much, but was much better than the streets.

At the camp, the older kids began to take some responsibility for the other kids, and gradually we developed a sense of order and structured programs.

Camp was costly but wonderful. By that time I had some helpers, and we took the kids out of the hood to see the country. Our lake house became summer camp headquarters as we watched sixty teens run and shout.

I never realized what a privilege it was to have space all our own. Our family had seven acres in the woods with 350 feet of lake frontage. We had enjoyed this escape from the city for years, and now I was able to share this with city kids who had never enjoyed that kind of freedom.

At first, the quiet bothered them. One of the girls, Angelina, said she was afraid of the openness and missed the noise of the city. One of the boys came running into the cabin wide-eyed with fear. He had never heard the sound of an owl hooting. Even the crickets and bullfrogs startled these city-bound kids!

Haskell Street

By the third year, Crusaders had grown quite large and the older children were bringing all their little brothers and sisters along. As we became increasingly involved in the lives of the children, we saw the need for residential space for the ones in crisis situations. Many nights, as we dropped one of our kids off at home, we found the mother incoherent due to drugs, or the apartment dark, empty, and the door locked. As our numbers increased and we needed more room, we moved a few blocks away to an old sandstone brick building on Haskell and Ross, where we soon hung our East Dallas Crusaders for Christ sign out front.

Dedication of facility: Morris Sheets (left); Dorothy and Ron Allen (center); Carolyn Smith (second from right)

Our meetings began in what used to be a bar on the first floor of the building. We had an enclosed courtyard in the back with a safe area for kickball games. Upstairs were a couple of bedrooms, a kitchen, and a living area. The neighborhood was typical of the day: crowded apartments with graffiti on the walls; frame houses with broken windows; and old cars, some with hoods that seemed forever raised.

The lot across from the building was full of idle men smoking joints and doing drug deals. Adjacent to our building was a hot tub prostitution club. Nights in our corner of Dallas were punctuated by loud music, laughter, screaming, and yelling from the prostitutes, drug dealers, and people who happened to call the place home.

That old sandstone building became a home to many of the at-risk kids in the neighborhood, with programs that included tutoring, Bible study, information on AIDS, drug abuse prevention, and various recreational activities. During our years on Haskell, we took care of different children in crisis situations overnight or as long as necessary. Pastor Willie, who by then lived in the area and worked with us, would stay with the kids.

Most of our children were with us for short-term stays, as we tried to place them in a safe house so somebody could take over their care.

One mother almost got violent with me as she determined that she was going to have custody over her kids, even though I told her I was going to step in and take custody of them. She said that under no circumstances could I get custody of her kids; she owned them. She and many parents like her only wanted custody in order to continue receiving the child welfare check, which they used to purchase drugs.

She eventually moved to South Dallas to get away from me, although she finally broke down one day and admitted that she needed help. I had prayed for her kids for years—a five-year-old boy, three-year-old girl, and an older brother. Their mother was a beautiful woman who used men to get whatever she wanted. Although she was the toughest woman I had ever worked with, she eventually came to the center, got help, trained as a dental assistant, and managed to turn her life around. The issues our kids were dealing with were serious. One boy came and confessed that his mother had forced him to have sex with their neighbor since age seven, and he didn't want to do it anymore.

Often, the younger kids were hired by the drug dealers to watch for the police and to warn their mothers when the police were doing a raid. One boy came to me and said, "I love my mother; I will do anything to help her. She is sick and needs drugs and I will help her any way I can." He was only six-years -old.

One night, his mother came into the kitchen stark naked and fell down in front of the refrigerator. The boy was crying and didn't know what to do.

We often caught kids at age five and six-years-old huffing on gasoline rags. They told us this helped them deal with the misery in their lives.

One day, a little three-year-old boy got hold of a penknife. I had never seen a child so angry. There was violence in his eyes. I couldn't get the knife out of his hand, so he jammed it into the light socket and sparks began to fly. The boy began to cry, and I picked him up and took him on my lap. He said he was angry that his mother was gone and he didn't have anybody.

Another little boy, Tony, came home from school to find his apartment boarded up with a

No Entry sign posted on the front door. Earlier in the day, the police took his mother off to prison for selling drugs. Neither the mother nor police considered the child. We took him in for a season until we could locate a neighbor to care for him. Larry, high school age; Farris, Larry's three-year-old brother; and their sister, Elizabeth were three of our kids. I always took the children home from Crusaders, but didn't always go upstairs with them. Their mother was usually high, and the children would stay at our center as long as we would allow them. Larry had assumed the role of father for the family and wouldn't tell me what was going on in the home. I knew the apartment building they lived in was a very dangerous place. I hated to take the kids home, as I knew that they were right back in hell the minute they got out of the van. I began to see that I needed to reach out to the single mothers in an attempt to offer some hope in their home situations. Doing so, we could more effectively help the children.

Many homeless people hung out on our roof and across the street in a vacant lot at our Haskell location. One of the homeless men sniffed gasoline and drank alcohol until he fried his brain. He deeply resented us moving into his territory and often would defecate, urinate, and write nasty notes on my car. We tried many times to help him, but he seemed too far gone to understand. He finally died of cirrhosis of the liver, right in front of the center.

Whenever we held service for the kids in that building, we inevitably heard sounds on the roof. The people hanging out across the street, selling and doing drugs under the dark cover of a patch of trees, came and slept their high off on the roof of our building. We had regular police raids on the place. My husband worried when I went down to that neighborhood. My attitude was that if the Lord had opened a door there, He would keep me perfectly safe in the midst of all the danger.

HELL HOUSE

During the years we were located on Haskell, we used the center to create Hell House, an evangelistic, Halloween centered drama. We decked out various rooms of our building in horrifying but realistic scenes: a woman crying over a dead man in a casket as a voice-over said, "It is appointed unto men once to die, but after this the judgment" (Heb 9:27); a drug scene with demons controlling the drugged individuals like marionettes; a domestic violence scene where a husband murders his wife while their son tries to intervene; a man in a shower who overdosed with a needle in his arm; and a suicide room with a voice-over saying, "You're worthless, get it over with" as a man puts a gun to his head and shoots himself. The kids came by the busloads, and we had lines a block long, looking for a thrill. Our motive was to show them the reality of hell and these lifestyles and offer an alternative to violence and drugs. Many asked to talk to a counselor afterwards. We prayed for them and invited them to Crusaders. Many came or joined one of the other free drug programs, like Victory Outreach or Care Center. Some of the men working the parking lot got propositioned by two women who worked at the hot tub club behind the building. The men invited the prostitutes to Hell House, paid their way in, and both of the women asked for prayer.

It was strange for our teens to see busses of kids from traditional churches scared because of the realness of the scenes we presented—scenes our inner-city kids experienced on a daily basis. Over four hundred people received prayer and help during Hell House.

THE GANG

During the early years, hundreds of kids passed through the doors of the Dallas Crusaders. Many stories were successes, while some ended with a distinct note of sadness.

One of our kids from the early years was Mario, a slim, eleven-year-old Hispanic boy whose nickname was Snoopy. I first met Snoopy in an alley and talked to him about coming to the Crusaders. Snoopy never let me come to his home. Instead, he met me in the street to take him and his sister to Crusaders. He was a handsome but terribly thin boy with a sunken chest from years of huffing on rags spiked with paint thinner. By the time I met him, he had already ruined one of his lungs. Snoopy was a natural leader who responded quickly to the outreach. He seemed to be making progress, but never totally left his old ways and lifestyle. There was a lot of gang activity in the neighborhood with the Crips and Bloods, and kids often joined one of the gangs for their own protection. The Crusaders became an alternative gang—a place of refuge from all the violence of the streets. The kids themselves made sure it stayed that way. We never had any major problems, although I have taken away many a knife or a handgun from some of the boys.

Snoopy was the leader of a local gang called the East Side Locos. One day, Snoopy decided to go for a ride in a car with another boy. When they crossed the border between the East Side Locos gang and the Wayne Street gang, Snoopy was gunned down and died instantly behind the wheel of the car.

Cookie Rodriguez and I did Snoopy's funeral service. During the funeral, there were dozens of FBI agents surrounding the funeral home. I shared briefly, asking the kids to find a way to live for Snoopy so that his life would have counted for something. I then watched in horror as the remaining gang members, wearing T-shirts with Snoopy's picture, each filed past his lifeless form and dropped a bullet into the open casket. The bullet symbolized that they would get even with the Wayne Street gang that was responsible for his death. Following the funeral, a large group of Hispanic kids started attending Crusaders. Chico was an older boy of nineteen when he joined Crusaders and quickly became my protector in the neighborhood. He would always park my car so the gangs would leave it alone. Once during a Crusader meeting, one of the boys got very ugly with me. As we left the meeting, I saw Chico swinging a car chain in front of him, telling the other boy in no uncertain terms to get off the territory.

Chico came from a large family with seven brothers and two sisters. Their father was an itinerant preacher who had abandoned his family and was in Mexico doing tent crusades. The kids made money any way they could. Life was hard, and they blamed the church for their problems and had become very bitter. I spent a lot of time in prayer and counseling with Chico and his brothers and helped them get past the bitterness. One night as we prayed together, Chico broke and all the pain and anger finally found a safe place to be released.

Unfortunately, he continued to play both sides of his life, and I believe he was involved with some dealers. He was eventually shot by the police in a raid at his apartment. When Chico died, his brothers asked me to perform the funeral.

I wanted so much to help the family and felt so

overwhelmed with the responsibility that I spent the next few days in prayer and fasting. When I stood before them that morning, I felt a deep sense of peace and began to share from my heart. I told them not to allow Chico's life to have been in vain, but reminded them that his life could be like a grain of wheat that had fallen into the earth; they could choose to bring forth new life from his loss.

I said, "This family can allow Chico's death to be an excuse to continue to lead destructive, hate-filled lives, or you can use his death as an opportunity to bring back the honor of your family name. If you will turn your lives over to Christ, He will give you the courage to change. All you have to do is ask for His help."

Most of Chico's brothers were older and into many things. In time, several of the brothers called me and asked me to pray for them to receive salvation and are now living useful, productive lives. I performed marriages for a couple of the boys and baptized some of the children. They have gone back to church, and Chico's younger brother, Raymond, went on to become a leader in the Crusaders and was the first member of his family to ever graduate from high school.

During the first year, we took Bernard from the Roseland Homes housing project, the other kids, and a ministry team from Christ for the Nations Institute on a retreat for a more in-depth time of ministry. To transport our Crusaders, we rented a van that had a unique and unfamiliar set of locks on the doors. While Bernard was exiting the van, someone slammed the passenger side door on his hand. In the midst of pandemonium, a screaming Bernard kept trying to unlock the door. My first thought was that this was the end of this ministry. I paused and asked for the Lord's help. Instantly the lock was released, and Bernard's hand, now white and flat like a pancake, was free.

I laid hands on Bernard's hand. As I prayed, Bernard stopped screaming as we literally watched his hand fill out and regain its natural color. All the kids in the van had seen the accident, and all of us realized we had witnessed a small miracle right in front of our eyes.

Bernard ended up being a faithful participant with the Crusaders from age nine through high school and over time developed into a strong leader.

That retreat was truly memorable. We had a special prayer service the first night and laid hands on all those who came. A big boy named Mark sauntered up to me for prayer with a very nasty attitude. When I laid my hand on his head, he literally fell backward on his rear end. He got back up off the floor and said, "What was that?" I told him the Lord wanted his attention and he replied, "Well He sure got it."

Mark was a changed young man after that and began to bring all his friends to Crusaders. I gave all the kids Living Bibles and the simple English helped them understand the love of God for them for the first time.

Another early Crusader leader was Chris, who,

now six feet nine inches tall, was always taller and larger than any of the other kids. From the beginning, Chris's authority was very apparent. He had no fear of the kids. He was able to stand up and tell them they needed to act like Christians. His love for the Lord was obvious in his life, and his love for the other kids was apparent. When he told them to jump, they jumped. He was the strongest influence in the Crusaders for four or five years.

Early crusader leaders: (rear, left to right) Salvador, Chris Nixon, Dorothy, Bernard, Isaac; (center) Nancy Beth

One of our guys, Raymond, developed pinkeye and came to the Crusaders with an inflamed red eye. During our meetings, I always had the kids pray, and Raymond's inflammation was an obvious need that people could see. I called Raymond to the front of the circle and rebuked the infirmity. As the night wore on and the program continued, Raymond's eye cleared up completely. The kids began to get excited in their faith as they saw God's power displayed. Raymond, like Chris, stayed with the Crusaders for many years. Outside the Crusaders and on the streets of east Dallas, these boys would have been enemies since Chris is black and Raymond Hispanic. But with the help of God, real friendships have been built and problems overcome over the years.

One night, one of the older boys came to tell us that some of the seven-and eight-year-old kids had decided to pull a heist. They had gotten a water pistol, marched from the projects to an Asian-owned T-shirt store, walked in on the proprietor, and put the toy pistol in his back. The man fainted, and the kids ransacked the store. As they walked back to the project, an older gang jumped them, beat them up, and took all the things they had stolen. The next day they all came to Crusaders looking way too innocent. I sat them in a circle and asked if anyone felt guilty and needed to confess something.

One of Nadine's sons, Leon, said, "Sister Dorothy, I gotta tell you something." The story all came out, and then he said, "It didn't work so good and we ended up losing everything that we stole. I think God was trying to teach us a lesson." Following their confession, I called the local juvenile officer and took the kids down to juvenile court. Most of the kids decided that it hadn't been a good idea to rob the store after that.

TRANSITION

I led the Crusaders for about twelve years. One evening in 1998, we had a lot of older kids from the projects attending the large group meeting. I could sense a rumble starting in the group and knew there was trouble brewing. This was a new group of kids and the potential for violence was greater than I had seen in the years prior. To get the troublemakers out of the place, I prayed and then looked at the kids and told the guys to go home or I would walk home with them and embarrass them in front of their friends. After I dealt with a potentially explosive situation and left the building, I knew that night was closure for my part in the ministry. I needed to find somebody younger to come in and take control of the group and build the ministry from there.

four

RECONCILIATION OUTREACH

$\mathbf{B}$y the the early 1990s, the ministry to east Dallas

had grown to include residential programs for men,

women, and families in need. A friend from Christ

For The Nations Institute introduced us to Hilton

Mansfield, a man from South Africa running a

men's program in Memphis. He was interested in

establishing a branch of his residential program for

men in our neighborhood. Together we worked out a way to share space at 1647 Haskell. The upstairs became apartments for the men, and we held services on different days in the large rooms downstairs. Carolyn Smith joined Reconciliation Outreach in 1993. Initially, we used my office at home for our planning sessions. With her help, the kids' programs began to develop a sense of order. Her bookkeeping skills brought structure to the organization where there had been none.

My early on-the-job training in residential ministry commenced when I was invited to take the role of Woman's Director for Mission Corp. On one of the trips to their headquarters in Memphis, I spent a great deal of time praying for various women in the ministry. One woman, Shelly, came up to me for prayer during the evening chapel service and immediately began to curse and scream at the top of her lungs. She was a very large woman, and five of the men from the mission promptly sat on her to bring her under control. As I began to pray for her, she rose up from the floor with such supernatural strength that she threw all of us in every direction as she ran out the front door.

Shelly ran to an old railroad track and lay down across the track in an attempt to commit suicide. We brought her back, and, after several hours of concentrated prayer, we saw her calm down enough that I was able to begin working with her. Our relationship continued for almost three years.

She eventually came to the Dallas area, entered our women's program, and currently is a successful nursing assistant living in her own town house.

Ministering to black women from the deep South, I was confronted with a culture that was a great shock to me. I had never seen women treated with such complete contempt. While this may not be true for many families, it was very common for those in our programs. The result of years of abuse was a palpable anger—often seen in violence and rage. Many of the women had been on drugs for so long they had developed symptoms similar to epilepsy, affecting their nervous system. The more I worked with the women, the more I began to realize that the movie *The Color Purple* represented a lifestyle that the vast majority of the women in our program had experienced.

I also found the same experience to be true in the lives of the majority of the women in our shelters. Somehow the terrible childhood abuse they experienced had taken its toll in such a way that many of the women had lost all sense of dignity and self-respect, to the point that nothing seemed to matter to them. They either became violently angry or self-destructive as a result of where they had been.

Obviously, since these women were the mothers of a generation of children, the kids that I worked with suffered the effects of their mother's pain. Only the grace of God has been able through the years to help us help them find a way out and begin life again. We have even witnessed and helped facilitate the restoration of children to single mothers who had to learn a whole new way of life for themselves and their children.

The relationship with Mission Corp worked well for three years, until they decided the women's and children's programs were too big a burden to carry. By that time we had leased a large building on Bryan Street with offices, a chapel, and an old burned-out restaurant.

I offered to move out of the facilities and began again with just the women and children's programs. We moved to an old warehouse down the street with very little money and no help in sight.

Eventually, Mission Corp moved out of the Bryan Street facility in late fall of 2000 and in 2001 closed its doors for good. We again took possession of the former Mission Corp property, and gradually, many of the leaders that had been with Mission Corp started coming to Reconciliation Outreach.

Robert Cook with early Women's leader Jackie

WINGS OF MERCY

Reconciliation Outreach's program for women began with a bang when I was asked to take over the Wings of Mercy, a program for women housed in an old apartment complex on Bryan Street. I was praying with Johnny Kennedy, the woman who ran the program, when the Lord told me that Johnny was going to ask me to take over the program. At the time, I had no idea what I was getting into.

We inherited fifty-two women in a house that was in terrible condition, including rotting floors and an infestation of rats eating out the walls. The city was constantly citing the property for various violations. Although the property was owned by a local foundation, we were responsible for all repairs and upkeep, even though we had no money.

There were drug dealers all around the vicinity of the house. They hung out in the alleyway behind the house and knocked the slats out in the fence so they could get to the women to sell them dope.

At the time we had a group of little kids in our daycare program called the Angels in the Hood. I had taught them a simple song about their authority as believers; that through Jesus, Satan was under their feet. As a demonstration of that truth, I asked them to write "Satan" on the bottom of their shoes and we marched around the neighborhood together singing and asking the Lord to get rid of the dealers.

Angels in the Hood

In answer to the children's faith, Dan Cruise, who owned the shopping center on the other side of the alley behind the house called me and told me that he heard about the trouble with the dealers. He offered to patrol the area and fence off the back alley to keep the dealers away. I took the children over there, and they watched as the police flushed the men out of the alley. The next day the fence was up.

We had the apartment complex on Bryan for about three years. The foundation then paid for a one-year lease on another apartment complex on San Jacinto while we raised the funds to build the apartment house called The Refuge. The house on Bryan was torn down almost immediately after we vacated and is now a parking lot.

I experienced another huge learning curve

taking over the Wings of Mercy program. I had never dealt with drugs and alcohol one-on-one before. Even the individual program leaders were recent addicts. Many women that I began with as leaders eventually lapsed back into the drug culture themselves, and we would have to start all over again.

When we took over the program, it consisted primarily of good intentions and a Bible study, with no set program or disciplinary structures in place. Mission Corp taught me some from their programs, although their emphasis was on getting jobs rather than cleaning out the inner man, while we utilized counseling and consistent, practical application of the Word of God to people's lives.

My experience has taught me that treating the whole man is most effective. In the beginning, all the adults need the transformed life that comes from spiritual training. During our program orientation they don't work in jobs to earn money; they are immersed in teaching, discipleship, and the practical aspects of changing their way of life.

After orientation, they are allowed to find work and begin to deal with their physical needs. The challenge with the men has always been that they desire to go to work immediately, struggling with taking the time to allow the Lord to heal them and help them sustain whatever job they get. Most are in too much of a hurry and don't allow time for the process to prepare them so they can eventually return to a stable lifestyle.

In raising up leaders from within the program, there is a mutual benefit. Many people from the street have heard the Word and been a part of the church at some point in their life but never made the relational connection with the Lord. We help them recognize their problems themselves and find comfort and acceptance within the small community. The love of the Lord is everywhere, and gradually they are able to let go of their anger and learn to trust.

A NEIGHBORHOOD TRANSFORMED

From our first step into residential ministry with the Wings of Mercy, the late 1990s saw Reconciliation Outreach expand the number of properties it occupied and the number of lives it touched. Two Dallas foundations provided significant grants to fund The Refuge, our facility for women and children. One of our board members, Bill Heard, wrote the grants to secure funding for our properties. Bill has been working like a bulldog on behalf of Reconciliation Outreach. Because of his tenacity, Reconciliation Outreach owns property currently worth millions of dollars.

The UPS Foundation chose us for a fifty thousand dollar grant, which allowed Tom Hardeman and a team of UPS retirees and young people from local churches to clean up a number of our properties, including a former drug house at 1508 Peak Street.

The years of drugs and the lifestyle of the people in

that apartment complex had taken its toll on the inside of the building. I remember the first time I walked in the door and found a naked couple asleep on a table by the door. The floor was covered with filth and the smell was impossible to describe. To even step inside the door required moving aside a deep pile of trash.

One prior occupant of 1508 Peak was one of the biggest drug dealers in the area. One afternoon I spotted him in the open field behind the apartments. He was soliciting some of the families in the neighborhood. Novelle Cook, an early Reconciliation Outreach staff member, and I walked over to him, looked him in the eye, and told him that he was hurting himself and others and the Lord wanted him to change his lifestyle.

I had watched him in the neighborhood over the years and had seen the damage in the lives of the people. I asked if he would let me pray for him. He broke down and said yes. As I prayed, the tough, hard expression on his face began to soften. When I finished, he said, "Lady, I'm not ready to quit what I'm doing, but I promise you one thing, I will get out of this neighborhood, and I will remember that I know how to live. One day I will maybe decide to change. In the mean time I promise you I will not come back to this part of the city."

When the presence of the Lord comes into an area, the changes take place not only in the lives of the people, but in the appearance of the property that they live in. The desire to clean up the inside of our lives seems to be reflected in the same way on the outside. The old crack houses that we took possession of were transformed from rundown, filthy housing to little Victorian homes with green picket fences. I am still amazed at the transformation that has taken place in our part of the hood.

Currently our ministry is providing food, clothing, and temporary housing for about 150 people and a total of seven hundred families and single adults each year through our life rehabilitation program. Our services include an in-house daycare for working mothers, after school tutoring for schoolchildren, Saturday activities for children, and a summer camp program.

Two ministry homes, each with house mothers, are designed for women who are trying to get on their feet. Many of them have been addicted to drugs; others have been abused and need a safe harbor. Reconciliation Outreach also has three men's houses, a children's building, a daycare center, and a nineteen-unit apartment building for individuals and families who need housing assistance until they can support themselves.

Chapel is held every day at noon and at night. Other programs offered at Reconciliation Outreach include share groups, personal growth groups, a Christian twelve-step program, one-on-one counseling, prison ministry, after-school programs, and business skills classes.

For many participants, one-on-one prayer time is crucial. Women who live in the homes are required to gather for prayer and worship every day at six o'clock in the morning. The men meet earlier to accommodate their work schedules. Approximately 80 percent of those who have gone through our six-month and one-year programs stay clean and are able to transition back into society as contributing members.

THE RESIDENTS

Most residents come to Reconciliation Outreach knowing that this is a mission focused on personal ministry. Individuals come because they are hungry for genuine change in their lives. A piece of their life is missing and they are looking for a place to restore their physical and inner self.

In Ezekiel 16:3–14, God describes His people as a helpless infant that was delivered and then abandoned before anyone washed the child, cut the umbilical cord, or swaddled her. God said, "And when I passed by you and saw you struggling in your own blood, I said . . . 'Live!'" (v. 6). The passage then describes how the Lord washed the child, anointed and cared for her, and made her of enviable beauty. These scriptures capture the essence of God's work at Reconciliation Outreach. When Reconciliation Outreach started, I recognized that God's motive was to minister to those who were so desperate, broken, and bleeding that, if left to themselves, they would literally die in their own blood. Anyone who comes here goes through a process of being healed of bitterness, alienation, or rebellion. They are loved in spite of their addictions, lifestyle, or appearance. Those that come broken and submit to the process are restored. Many who come into our programs are not quite ready to change, so they struggle and have to go through a lot of pain. Fortunately for all of us, the one thing that brings us all to change is that when we are up against enough pain, we are forced to make a change.

Every kind of safety measure is in place at Reconciliation Outreach to protect individuals against their own self-destructive behavior. Residents enter the program and the rules almost put the flesh in chains, keeping them from doing the things that have destroyed their minds and bodies. During their stay with the mission, we try to nourish the inner man of our residents so the Lord can sustain them once they are through the program. For many we become like a second family if the first was not able to provide the discipline and training for them to develop. Many individuals live in an adult body, but function like a child: unhappy and immature. We help them face that reality and change.

The Bible says that if we abide in God's Word, we will be His disciples and that "you shall know the truth, and the truth shall make you free" (John 8:31–32). It is the recognition of truth by our personal experience that causes us to change. The people who succeed in the program are like the prodigal son who woke up one day, recognized his self-destructive behavior, and decided to return home. We hope to be like the prodigal's father and accept him or her as he or she is, while we offer help to find a new way. (See Luke 15:11–24.)

The residents of Reconciliation Outreach are a microcosm of our world, but circumstances have forced them to make changes in their lifestyle. Most of them have lost all family ties and are financially unable to support themselves.

In ministry we realize that the emphasis has to be on the truth. As long as we are deceived that we are "nice," we never face up to what may be hidden on the inside. Coming to the awareness of our real condition and need and acknowledging that need can take time.

In many ways, Reconciliation Outreach is like a hospital. Most residents who are successful need at least six months at the mission, although they can stay long-term if they need the support system. It took many years to mess their lives up, and it is a slow healing process to get their lives back in order. If a resident's family situation and support system is in a shambles, they do better staying here, getting jobs, joining the church, and remaining a part of the community.

Several of the early women ended up leaving

the program and stumbling back into their old lifestyles. All have recovered and managed to turn their lives back around. Even their commitment to Christ and their transformation as Christians weren't always able to carry them through their crisis. In many cases, it took them years to overcome. Many of these women, now leaders, helped teach me the terrible effects of addiction on a person's life. Many Christians believe that once you receive Christ you will never struggle with addiction. The truth is that the addiction entered in when the person lacked character, strength, or self-discipline. Because they lacked self-discipline, they used drugs as an escape from their problems. People need more than just spiritual transformation; they need the character development that forms over time.

Dorothy and Carliss Talton

RECONCILIATION CHURCH

While ministry is usually birthed out of a church, Reconciliation Outreach was a church long before it was called one. From our inception, we had all the components of the church—the spiritual emphasis, service, and outreach to the community—without the name.

My husband was a trustee of Hillcrest Church, and we were both active in the work of that church, so we began to transport all our residents there on Sundays. Pastor Willie Burnett organized a caravan consisting of all available and running vans and cars to drive our residents to Hillcrest Church every Sunday.

Dorothy and Pastor Willie Burnett

The sweet part of the Reconciliation Outreach relationship with Hillcrest Church was seeing the cross-cultural love that took place between a primarily white church and the primarily minority group from Reconciliation Outreach. To keep the identity of Reconciliation Outreach, my husband and I, Pastor Willie, and Ron and Pat Allen held a worship and prayer service in the chapel before joining the main service at eleven o'clock. The cross-cultural impact was noticeable from the first visit when one lady from church came and asked me, "Where are all the homeless people?"She did not expect the residents from Reconciliation Outreach to be clean, well-dressed, and look like everybody else.

Reconciliation Outreach has had some of the best con-artists in the world in our program. At first, these same cons went to work on the sweet little ladies in the church, asking for money to meet their needs. The Reconciliation Outreach kids who had never been trained were brought into the middle of the well-trained Hillcrest kids in Sunday school. The first week, our kids ate up all the donuts and stole the money from the coffee donation's cup. Even so, gradually, real friendships developed between the church members and those from the Reconciliation Outreach.

Overall, the years at Hillcrest bore fruit in bringing two diverse cultures—inner-city poor and suburban, privileged white—together as two parts of a whole. The problem was not the color of our skin but the difference between the levels of discipline and training in the youth. My job became that of a mediator as I worked with both sides to solve problems. Out of necessity, we eventually started Reconciliation Church in our chapel. Sundays had become a major transportation headache for us, and we could no longer afford the expense of carrying 150 people to Hillcrest Church each Sunday. Worship is the center of everything here at Reconciliation Outreach. All our leaders understand the important part that worship plays in the ministry. From the first day, the anointing has been sweet over our ministry times. The church service where we come together as a body has become the continuation and culmination of the week.

The church has a great potential for growth, and in time it will need a new building. With a growing cross-cultural Spanish speaking team led by Roberto Espinoza and his son, I believe that Reconciliation Outreach Church will become a much larger bilingual congregation, similar to the Dream Center in Los Angeles, California.

We are located in the heart of the city, serving the racially, culturally and economically diverse peoples that live in our part of the hood.

LORD, SEND ME A MAN!

By 2004, I had reached a crisis point. The weight of responsibility for the ministry had become a burden that I was feeling increasingly ill-equipped to carry.

I never doubted that the ministry should continue, but wasn't sure of the form that it should take. I am a firm believer that God guides us through finances. When there is not enough money, it is important to ask God why the cash flow is tight. Through the years, God has never given Reconciliation Outreach great amounts of money, or one individual who would give a big gift. However, provision always came through regular staff prayer and private times, where we would lay before the Lord for hours waiting for the answer. God simply heard our cries and answered them. I can honestly say that each property, every individual in ministry, and all financial blessings have been in answer to persistent prayer, despite things looking hopeless.

For two years before our current director, Leonard Brannon, came to the ministry, I asked the Lord to send a man with the same heart for ministry and with the gift of administration, so there could be order in the house. Though I worked hard at administration, I didn't use my lack of experience as an excuse to not try new things. Although I tried to govern wisely and keep things in order, I knew that long-term I had to have somebody with vision and wisdom to maintain the work and allow it to grow.

When God started adding numbers to the ministry back in the early 1990s with explosive growth, I had a long night of argument with the Lord. I lay on the floor and told the Lord that my heart was that of a mother, able to put my arms around what I had. I knew that if the ministry got too big, it would outgrow my capacity to lead it. I told the Lord that if His direction was to grow this ministry, He would have to draw in those that would be able to bring order. Confirmation came through several intercessors and a scripture I read that described how the Lord sent to David those that were armed, trained, and ready for war. I also needed those who came alongside me to be armed, trained, and called to war. I knew that God had a man to lift the stress of carrying the burden that was on my shoulders for twelve overwhelming years.

Leonard Brannon, a longtime friend and fellow missionary to the inner city, called and told me he made a decision that it was time to release his prior organization, Care Center. He believed that he was called to start another church and wanted to pray with me about direction for the future.

It all seemed so easy after that—there was no second thought in either of our minds. There was an instant bond with Leonard, with both of us having great hearts desiring to help the poor. For me, there was no need to hang on to what I had, as it was a natural flow to release the reigns of authority into Leonard's hands, knowing the flow was continuing. In the midst of the transition, Leonard has shown grace in continuing to work with me, keeping me as a part of the heart of the mission, working in a noncompetitive way.

THE FUTURE

My arms have been stretched way beyond their ability as the ministry continues to grow. I wake up every morning with excitement, wondering what new thing the day will bring. My husband, Bob, retired from the legal profession last year, and we built a lovely Spanish-style home in the country near Dallas so we could enjoy the best of both worlds. Bob and I enjoy the outdoors together, and we spend our time with our children, grandchildren, and extended family as often as possible.

I have an apartment at the mission and often stay there to avoid the long drive home. Bob and I both enjoy the church services at the mission, and I have remained actively involved in teaching and prayer as well as planning the future for Reconciliation Outreach with the board and Pastor Brannon.

The Moore Family

I recognize the seriousness of the times we live in, but I continue to trust in the God who has been with me all these years. He has allowed me to follow Him into things that were impossible to me and has stretched me beyond my natural abilities. Only He knows the future, and I am content to trust Him with mine. My only job is to stay faithful in the relationship with Him and with those He has sent across my path.

The mission today remains the same, but the value of the work continues to increase with the value of the land it sits on. The ministry owns a large chunk of real estate in Dallas and continues to serve the growing needs of the poor. The housing and Christian programs provide a sense of stability to the area once occupied by several rival gangs and a thriving drug trade.

The crack houses are being replaced by our safe homes, where no alcohol or drugs are allowed. The children are protected and carefully supervised by the staff and the residents, who take personal interest in their lives.

With the addition of our lovely new apartment building, we provide the next step for those who complete our training programs. The low-cost rental units are available after residents find full-time employment.

Leonard Brannon and Dorothy Moore

Our property on Peak Street is now debt free. All the housing is fully occupied, with a waiting list. Reconciliation Scholars Academy, our new charter school will open its doors next fall to eventually serve 550 kids who otherwise might have fallen through the cracks in our public school system. Leonard Brannon and others did all the hard work and have allowed me to share in the birthing of the school. As one of only eleven charter schools out of five hundred chosen—and the only one in Dallas— we have had great favor from the state Board of Education and encouragement from all sides.

While charter schools are paid for by the state, they must provide their own facility. As we stepped out in faith with our eye on the three-story Brannon Building, adjacent to our current office, God provided! The 115 Brannon Building was purchased for us as a

Christmas present, and the first classes were held in the fall of 2007. The school is the fulfillment of a dream I have carried in my heart for twenty years, and it will enable us to make a huge difference for thousands of inner-city kids and families for years to come.

five

LIFE MESSAGES

The biggest dilemma I have faced as a woman in ministry has been reconciling the call God has placed on my life with my roles as wife and mother, while acknowledging the sacredness of my womanhood. Every woman has to struggle with this question, and I spent a great deal of time in prayer asking the Lord what He expected of me. Because of my dramatic conversion experience, I felt that there was a very particular thing that I was to do with all the opportunities and blessings I had received. In the beginning, I had very little clarity about how to use what I had. It wasn't until we returned to Dallas the second time that I began to bring together all the resources that I had been given to the Lord to be used in ministry. I have learned that it is not what I am doing, but what He wants to do that is important.

STEPPING INTO THE DEEP

When the Lord called me to inner city ministry, it didn't make sense. I was completely out of my comfort zone. I enjoyed ministry to women, and that seemed a natural fit for me. Here I was, taken out of the security of a church environment and thrown into something foreign. I was completely in over my head! To calm my fears, the Lord showed me a picture of myself down at the seashore wearing life jackets from neck to feet. As I got close to the water and stepped in, I couldn't put my feet into the water because I had to take the life jackets off. I took off the jackets, got into the water up to my knees and was okay. I got in the water up to my shoulders and, amazingly, could still stand. Suddenly, I had nowhere to put my feet. I had stepped off into the deep and had nothing to stand on. All I could do was float.

I realized that if God were going to do this ministry in the inner city through me, He would show me how to do it. I first had to remove the security that the life jackets afforded, and step out into the deep in faith that with His care and support I would not drown, but float.

As I learned total dependence on God, prayer became the foundation of my life, birthing all the transitions and ministry. All through the years it has been the voice and grace of God that has personally guided me and allowed me to build the foundation for a very strong inner city ministry. Suddenly being launched into something this large and ministering cross-culturally among the poor was something that I was totally unqualified for. Obviously I wasn't a woman of color or from a background of poverty. It took me a long time to get beyond apologizing for who I was: white, a woman, and wealthy. I honestly thought that the very people I was reaching out to would reject me. I understood their pain in my head, but I had never walked in their shoes. It took much time alone with the Lord to get His direction and wisdom for what was needed in the ministry.

While I felt like an outsider in the culture I was called to, people in my own culture thanked me for not making them feel guilty for where I was in ministry. One reason I believe the Lord was able to use me is that the people coming to the ministry knew that I had nothing to gain from them. So many had been used by those they trusted. Because there was no reason for me to con or use them, they learned to trust me.

In the early years, I was consumed and weary, working with something that kept getting bigger and bigger. In the midst of a very difficult time, several friends "kidnapped" me and drove to a retreat in Arkansas called The Little Portion. When they parked the car, I got out and just fell down face-first in the green grass. All the pressure I was feeling began to lift as I spent the weekend there all alone. By the time Monday came I was ready to tackle all the problems back home.

The work of ministry never ends, but I have learned to step away from the stress and rest, knowing that this is a marathon and not the one-hundred-yard dash. My husband and family have always been there for me and help me keep my balance.

GOD THE EQUIPPER

I may never understand why I am here in the inner city, but I trust He knows where to place me for greatest fruitfulness in His kingdom.

Early in ministry I realized my great need to grow up and become the kind of person God could use. It took God a long time and a lot of patience. Fortunately, He is just as concerned at developing the character of a leader as He is that the leader teaches the flock. In the beginning, I felt totally inadequate for the job. I deeply loved the kids and prayed for them daily, but felt I lacked so many things they needed. Somehow the kids overlooked the things I worried about and responded to the love and consistent program we continued to offer. Over time, the Lord gave me confidence to teach the Word. I teach the whole mission on Tuesday nights and look forward to our time together. I believe they are just like me inside. They want their life to count in some way. They want to make a difference in this life, and I preach to that need. Nobody starts out to be a failure in life or to be a criminal or a drug addict, and they need God's help to change their lives.

As our programs grew, I gradually realized that it was not a matter of being the right color or sex; it was either that the Lord was Lord of the work, or He wasn't. The effectiveness was not limited to the person in the job. I did not set limits on God for Reconciliation Outreach, so God could repeatedly do with me what He wanted. It was through that faith-walk that the ministry was built from scratch.

I believe God equipped me in a manner similar to Corrie Ten Boom, who was called to obey God but only got the direction and provision that she needed right before it was necessary. God has equipped me to do everything He has called me to do! And, as the Lord allowed brokenness into my own life, I have learned to submit to Him and to others.

A Servant's Heart

When I was putting the ministry together, I had several local leaders who approached me with methods they thought I should use. They believed they could come down to the inner city and fix the problems of the people, while I instinctively realized that was not the answer. The Lord showed me that people's dignity mattered to Him. He had given these people the ability to struggle through their problems, and that they had a great deal they could teach me if I humbled myself and served alongside them instead of trying to solve all of their problems for them.

Many of us who have never lived in an inner city environment want to put a box over the problem and fix it. But the problem needs the people who see the problem and those who live in the problem to work together in order to join suburban and inner-city resources and change the situation.

I came to serve alongside the people who are poor and needy. Many times they are put in circumstances beyond their control and a hand-up is all they needed. Gradually the ministry began to take on a personality of its own, and a deep bond developed between us as we began to rebuild their neighborhood one brick at a time.

The problem on both sides is pride. Pride seems to be the one thing the Lord has always hated the most. Overtime I began to recognize pride in my own life and in others. Many times the pride is unconscious, accepting a superiority that we thought we had, that God never intended us to walk in. At the cross, Jesus became our equalizer. All of us are called as servants.

Through the years I have learned a great deal about wealth and power and how they could be used for good or to destroy. With our lack of sensitivity and understanding of other people's lives, we, even with the best of intentions, can create more problems than we solve.

Early on, the Lord showed me what my primary assignment for Him was—to act as a bridge that those who had the wealth, knowledge, and blessing could walk over to reach those in need, and vice versa. I have seen Him help me build that bridge, which I believe is the meaning of the scripture in 2 Corinthians 5:18: "Now all things are of God, who has reconciled us to Himself through Jesus Christ, and has given us the ministry of reconciliation." Since my life has been changed by God's love, He expects me to become that bridge, that others may come to know His love through me.

Reconciliation requires sacrifice. Philippians says that Christ came as a servant; He sacrificed His right as God to become the way of reconciliation for us to God. (See Philippians 2:7.) He then taught us to be servants to others so that they might find their way back to God. It is a very simple thing, but learning to live that way is not simple. Instead, it requires a lifetime of seeking His way and not our own. If you model servant hood in ministry, you produce servants. That is the model I have tried to provide. I have learned some badly needed humility in the process. As a servant, I recognized I no longer had a right to certain things, but had to ask like everyone else for what I needed. I was serving in the same way others did.

THE NEEDY

Early on, I discovered while working with those who have never had anything that the needy may be so desperate to seek provision for their needs that they can quickly deplete the physical and emotional resources of those providing them assistance. I was reminded of when I was a lifeguard as a teenager. A man went off the high board and collided with another man underwater. The man was panicked and crawling on my shoulders trying to get his head above water to breathe. He was much bigger than me and almost took us both down. I had to sock him in the jaw to calm him down and get him out of the water. That man was like so many who desperately want to get out of their circumstances. I had to learn how to help people without allowing them to drown me in the process.

I remember a time in my life when I began to feel rather pleased with myself. I wanted to be like a trophy in a display case and smile at the world so all could admire what the Lord had done in me. Then I thought about all the people who have loved me and helped me to grow up and all the things they had put up with. They had sacrificed many things to be there for me, and now it was my turn to do the same for others.

Judson Cornwall used the following story at a speaking engagement at Christ For The Nations International in October of 1981 to illustrate the process of refinement. He said a stone that God had worked on and placed in the wall He was building was pleased with himself until God put another stone with a very sharp, protruding edge right on top of him. The first stone expected God to smooth the other's rough edge, when instead the Lord cut out a wedge in him so the other rock could fit. I suppose most of us would like to fix the other guy rather than making room for him by giving up a piece of ourselves.

Through the ministry, God taught me that things He has worked on in my life have to be tested by others. If I sit on the shelf or in the display case, I am no longer useful. If I get out of the case and risk being sometimes used by others, I will be useful in the kingdom. The choice between being used and useful will always be there. Being useless is not something any of us really want. I found that although I was used in many ways, it all flowed in and through me; what was taken from me was always given back by the Lord. It didn't hurt me to be used.

As part of the Christian's growth, we understand that we will be used by God and by man. Although it is painful at times, it is the only way that we grow. We become more like Jesus when we understand what suffering really is.

MESSAGE TO THE CHURCH

The streets are as hard as the concrete they're made of, and the homelessness is more a matter of the heart than a lack of a place to sleep. The simple truth is: many are homeless because the spark of life has been turned down so low that they have lost all hope. Survival and drugs that dim reality become everything. Relationships are abandoned; they lose their place within families as the addiction takes over or they become a terrible burden to those who are family in name only.

"Jesus loves me this I know," is the church's expression of that simple childlike need we all share to belong, to matter, to be loved. This love heals. This unconditional love covers and forgives the past. This love believes that His mercies are new every morning" (Lam. 3:23). Love, the agape kind of love, changes the one who lives by it and the one to whom it is given. This is why real emotional healing is best found within the heart of those who have received it themselves. Paul's challenge to the Christian is to not be overcome by evil but to overcome evil with good (Rom. 12:21).

As we reach out to these nameless, faceless people, we will have to learn tough love. God's love gives everything, but He expects nothing less from us than total surrender. He says clearly, "He who comes to God must believe that He is, and that He is a rewarder of those who diligently seek Him" (Heb. 11:6). But He also says, "He who does not take his cross and follow after Me is not worthy of Me. He who finds his life will lose it, and he who loses his life for My sake will find it" (Matt. 10:38–39).

We, as the church in today's world, must be willing to lay down our lives for others. If we choose to live as He lived, He will be lifted up, and His Word promises He will draw all men unto Himself (John 12:32).

We find home when we find Him. God becomes our Father, and His body—the church—becomes our sisters and brothers. Christ is the perfect older brother that models for us how to be a family. We as sisters and brothers represent Him today, and we must be willing to open our lives to others and say, "Follow me as I follow Christ."

The church can only help change the inner city when she becomes a visible presence to the inner city world. She must come as a servant. Our young people must see examples of sacrifice. We must look more like Christ and less like the world around us.

God's two commands to us are to love Him with all our hearts and to love our neighbors as ourselves. (See Matthew 22:37–39; Mark 12:30–31; Luke 10:27.) If we choose to stand outside and judge others, we become part of the problem. God will have to deal with us. We all need grace, first from God and then from each other. If I stay full of Him instead of me, I become a transforming agent, drawing people to the source.

A call is going out across our land: "Come and help us." The inner cities cry out for the strong, and the Holy Spirit is at work in the church to awaken the sleeping giant. A pastor friend once shared a story with me that I will always remember:

> I had taken my family for a walk. We had gone several blocks and suddenly realized Sharon was not with us. I looked back and spotted her standing, crying a block behind us. I called her to come catch up, but she only began to weep harder and managed a muffled, "I can't, Daddy. I just can't." With that, I went back to where she stood, took her by the hand, and led her to where the rest of the family waited. You see, Sharon is mentally retarded and although she wanted to keep up, she needed a hand.

The church family is a lot like that. We receive the salvation experience and all the wonderful gifts and training the Lord gives to His children. Then we run to the front of the pack and compete with one another over positions and recognition within the church community. We have forgotten the poor among us, the addicts, the prisoners, the mentally slow, those who are trapped within the walls of our inner cities. The biggest problem in today's local church is distance. The suburban church is unable to understand the pain of the inner city church because they are not connected together. Many have grown too comfortable in their churches and neighborhoods and are insulated from the needs of the inner city. Most people find out it's not difficult once they come down to the inner city. They find it's a pleasure and a privilege, reaching out to God's people. When you're living on the frontlines, you see God doing such wonderful things. How exciting to allow God to use you in a way that makes you feel you are a part of something so much bigger than yourself!

THE MEANING OF RECONCILIATION

I see a parallel between the reconciliation of the Jew and Gentile in Christ and the reconciliation of races and cultures in our time. The problems are not the same, but the answer Paul offered is.

> For He is our peace, who hath made both one, and hath broken down the middle wall of partition between us … to make in himself of twain one new man, so making peace; And that

He might reconcile both unto God in
one body by the cross, having slain
the enmity thereby.

—Ephesians 2:14–16, KJV

The Christ that came as an obedient servant provides the only bridge able to reconcile us. Our differences are very real—social, economic, who controls the power. Offenses are deep and too obvious to be ignored. They can only be healed by those willing to lay down their pride, their bitterness, and their right to judge one another.

Reconciliation cost Jesus His life. We, as His servants, must be willing to pay the price. Reconciliation costs both sides, and there is no room for pride. As we serve one another faithfully, we will earn the right to be heard.

A number of years ago, our pastor at the time asked me to represent the church on a planning committee for a conference on inner city ministry. I attended the first meeting and realized I was the only white woman and the only charismatic in the room. The atmosphere in the room was cold. I perceived they were not receptive to working with me. When it was my turn to speak, I said, "I feel very much like the prodigal son who sought the gifts from the Father and consumed them on my own pleasure. But I have come back to the Father desiring to serve alongside my elder brother, only to find I am not welcome." The atmosphere in the room began to warm up a little, and we managed to find common ground to work together for the Father.

Our inner cities cry out for reconciliation, but like many of us, pride and bitterness freeze the words on their tongue. The suburban church pulls further and further away from the problems, wanting to help but finding themselves paralyzed by fear and self-preservation. No welfare program has ever been able to heal the problems of the heart. The church as a whole can only change the inner city when she becomes a visible presence to the inner city world. She must come as a servant.

Long ago, Moses gave up the pleasures of his comfortable position of power in Egypt to reach out to the people of God and to lead them out of slavery. The Jews of his day did not welcome him with open arms, and neither will the lost prodigals of today. When all they ever knew was slavery, how could they trust those who came in the Lord's name to offer freedom?

God's call to us is the same today— "Let the oppressed go free" (Isa. 58:6, KJV).

John 3:17 (KJV) reminds us, "For God sent not his Son into the world to condemn the world; but that the world through him might be saved." The ground has always been equal at the Cross. We stand together there not because we earned His forgiveness by our righteousness or our social position, but because we are covered by His grace.

NOTES

Definitions

1. Merriam-Webster's Dictionary Online, s.v. "lady," http://www.merriam-webster.com/dictionary/lady (accessed February 14, 2008).

2. The Online Slang Dictionary, s.v. "hood," http://onlineslangdictionary.com/definition+of/hood (accessed February 14, 2008).

TO CONTACT THE AUTHOR

To contact Dorothy Moore for speaking engagements:

> E-mail: dorothyrom@gmail.com;
> Phone (214) 536-5812

To order additional copies of this book:

> www.ladyinthehood.com

To find out additional information on Reconciliation Outreach or to make a financial donation:

> Reconciliation Outreach
> 4311 Bryan Street
> Dallas, TX 75204
> E-mail: Changinglives@rodallas.org
> Phone: (214) 821-9192

To support Reconciliation Outreach in prayer:

Pray that we will reach out in love to overcome racial divisions and fears (Gal. 5:13).

Pray that our city/country becomes a testimony of Christian love and mercy (Luke 4:5-8).